I0146001

The Future of Canada's Territorial Borders and Personal Boundaries

S.D. Clark

The University of Toronto's Department of Sociology was established in 1963. Samuel Delbert (S.D.) Clark (1910–2003) was its founding chair.

Clark was born in Lloydmister, Alberta, and attended the University of Saskatchewan, the London School of Economics, McGill University and the University of Toronto. He analyzed the transformation of successive Canadian frontiers from socially disorganized settlements into organized societies. He then conducted research on how economic change in Canada resulted in inequality as reflected in patterns of residential segregation. His books include *The Canadian Manufacturers Association* (1939), *The Social Development of Canada* (1942), *Church and Sect in Canada* (1948), *Movements of Political Protest in Canada* (1959), *The Developing Canadian Community* (1962), *The Suburban Society* (1966), *Canadian Society in Historical Perspective* (1976) and *The New Urban Poor* (1978).

Clark served as president of the Canadian Political Science Association, honorary president of the Canadian Sociology and Anthropology Association and president of the Royal Society of Canada. He was awarded the J.B. Tyrell Historical Medal, became a foreign honorary member of the American Academy of Arts and Sciences and an Officer of the Order of Canada, and received honorary degrees from half a dozen Canadian universities.

In 1999, Clark's son, William Edmund (Ed) Clark, endowed the S.D. Clark Chair in Sociology at the University of Toronto in honour of his father.

The Future of Canada's Territorial Borders and Personal Boundaries

PROCEEDINGS OF THE THIRD
S.D. CLARK SYMPOSIUM
ON THE FUTURE OF CANADIAN SOCIETY

EDITED BY
Robert Brym

Rock's Mills Press
Oakville, Ontario
2018

PUBLISHED BY

ROCK'S MILLS PRESS

www.rocksmillspress.com

Copyright © 2018 by Robert Brym
All rights reserved. Published by arrangement with the editor.

Cover: This map presents a comprehensive view of hypothetical continental shelf claims (for Canada and the US), submitted claims (for Denmark and Russia), and approved claims (for Iceland and Norway), as well as the constraint lines used for determining the limits of continental shelf claims. Additionally, the map indicates internal waters, territorial seas, and exclusive economic zones for each of the Arctic coastal states, special areas within exclusive economic zones, and the one area of dispute in the Arctic Ocean (in the Beaufort Sea, between the US and Canada). The map is reprinted with permission of IBRU: Centre for Borders Research, Durham University, United Kingdom. Please visit http://www.durham.ac.uk/ibru/resources/arctic to view the briefing notes that accompany the map.

For information, contact customer.service@rocksmillspress.com.
Library and Archives Canada Cataloguing in Publication data is available from the publisher.

Contents

List of Figures

The Future of Canada's Territorial Borders and Personal Boundaries

INTRODUCTION

CHAPTER ONE

The Future of Canada's Territorial Borders and Personal Boundaries[1]

Robert Brym

It has become customary to open public events at the University of Toronto with the following statement:

> We wish to acknowledge this land on which the University of Toronto operates. For thousands of years it has been the traditional land of the Huron-Wendat, the Seneca, and most recently, the Mississaugas of the Credit River. Today, this meeting place is still the home to many Indigenous people from across Turtle Island and we are grateful to have the opportunity to work on this land.

Recognizing our indebtedness to the original human inhabitants of the territory on which we work and reside puts us in an ideal frame of mind for the subject of this symposium. It reminds us that political borders and personal boundaries, and therefore control over territory and one's very self, are not fixed. Territorial borders and personal boundaries are always contested and thus, to varying degrees, fluid.

Thinking across territory and time, we observe instances of relatively stable and of relatively viscous borders. We rarely see the kind of rapid and wholesale border change that the once-powerful Polish-Lithuanian Commonwealth underwent between 1772 and 1795, when Prussia and the Austrian and Russian Empires devoured successively large chunks of the Commonwealth until it no longer existed as an independent entity, a condition it endured for 123 years (Figure 1.1). Change in the self-identification of many of its citizens followed; only in Galicia, the Austrian-controlled province, did a sense of Polish autonomy remain strong in cultural matters (Nance 2008: 1). But if this example is exceptional, territorial disputes, some

1. The Third S.D. Clark Symposium was sponsored by the S.D. Clark Chair of Sociology, University College, and Canada's Sesquicentennial Initiatives Fund, all at the University of Toronto.

loud, others muted, nonetheless remain the norm. A map that paints the countries that are today involved in a territorial dispute with at least one other country displays a sea of contention (Figure 1.2). China leads the list of disputants, engaged as it is in territorial disagreements with Taiwan, North Korea, South Korea, Japan, Bhutan, India, Vietnam, Philippines, Malaysia, and Brunei. Rare is the case of Bir Tawil, a remote and uninhabited area along the border between Egypt and Sudan about 3.25 times the area of the City of Toronto. It is claimed by no one (Figure 1.3).

The papers in Section 1 of this collection set the stage—theoretically, comparatively and globally—for the Canadian case studies that follow. John Hannigan from the Department of Sociology at the

Figure 1.1.
The Partitions of Poland, 1772–95
Polish territory in white, bordered by bold line

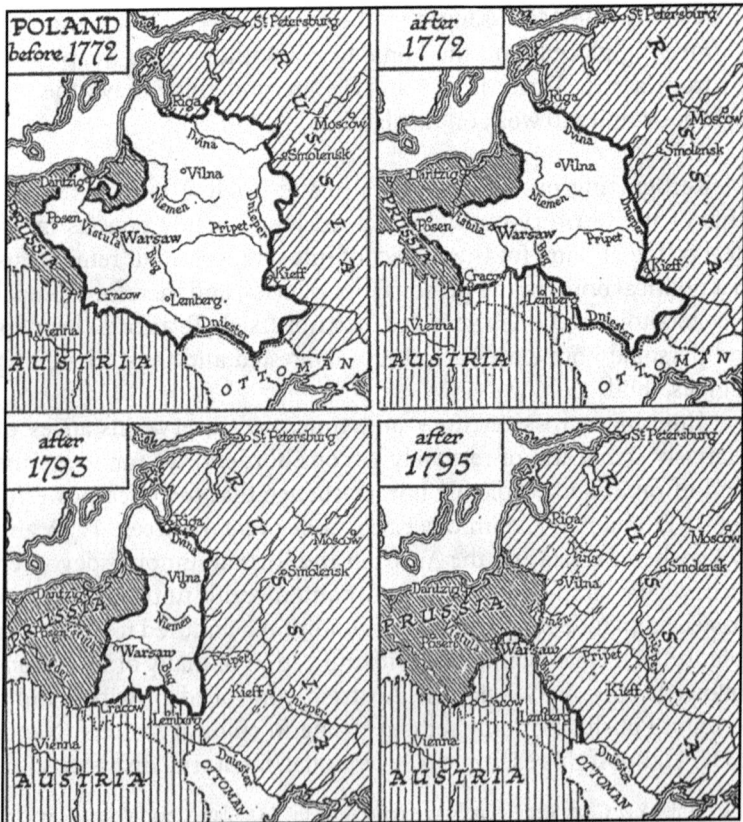

Source: Wells (1920).

University of Toronto initiates our journey by reminding us that recent debate in the field of border studies has focused on whether borders and boundaries are becoming more permeable due largely

Figure 1.2.
Countries with at Least One Territorial Dispute, 2015
Countries shaded in dark grey have at least one dispute underway.

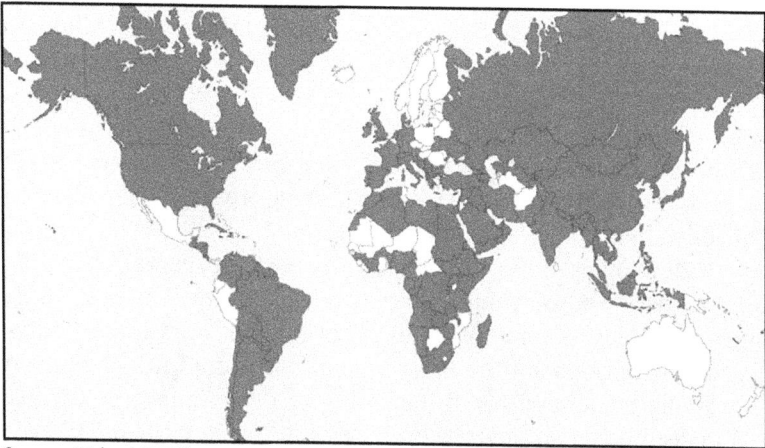

Source: Hielord (2015).

Figure 1.3. Bir Tawil Claimed by No One

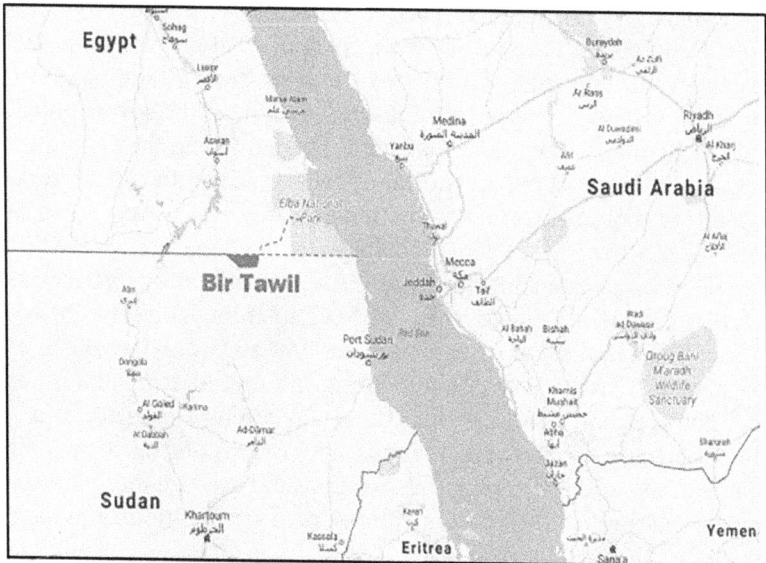

Source: Adapted from Google Maps (2017).

to globalization or more impermeable due largely to the heightened security concerns of sovereign states.

My view is that the arguments put forward on both sides of this debate are tendentious if not teleological. Technologies may allow State A to strengthen its control and extend its reach by means of surveillance, censorship and hacking. However, the very same technologies routinely allow elements of global civil society (not to mention State B) to subvert those efforts, at least to a degree (Brym et al. 2014; Brym et al. 2018). Accordingly, if we look closely, it is difficult to discern a universal tendency toward either more or less permeability because, as Michel Foucault (1977 [1975]; 1981 [1976]) insists, every exercise of power is subject to resistance, the outcome of which is shrouded in uncertainty. Or as Shakespeare (1595) famously put it, even "the smallest worm will turn, being trodden on," and even "doves will peck in safeguard of their brood."

Technological innovation has increased the degree to which *all* territorial and personal spaces (except Bir Tawil) have become sites of contention for control. In my opinion, if we want to understand why borders and boundaries shift, we should not assume an inexorable tendency toward increasing or decreasing permeability but instead focus on how the exercise of power in particular places breeds resistance, thus causing territorial and personal borderlands to change in shape, operation, and structure.[2]

And that is just what the scholars whose works are assembled here manage to accomplish, each in his or her own way. Professors Ron Deibert and Louis Pauly from the University of Toronto's Department of Political Science recognize how, during the first dozen or so years of its existence, the Internet challenged the sovereign authority of states. They note that states reacted to the threat by subsequently seeking to re-territorialize cyberspace and project power outside of their territorial jurisdictions. However, the story does not end there. One way in which civil society is energetically resisting state and corporate control efforts is through efforts by institutions such as Professor Deibert's own Citizen Lab at the University of Toronto. The Citizen Lab is dedicated to "investigating digital espionage against civil society, documenting Internet filtering and other technologies and practices that impact freedom of expression online, analyzing privacy, security, and information controls of popular applications, and examining transparency and accountability mechanisms relevant to the relationship between corporations and state

2. For an illustration of this approach, see Gordon's (2008) analysis of the Israeli occupation of the West Bank.

agencies regarding personal data and other surveillance activities" (Citizen Lab 2017). The chapter by Professors Deibert and Pauly illustrates the rich accomplishments of this work.

Professor Klaus Dodds of Royal Holloway, University of London, next analyzes the competition between Russia, the United States, Denmark, Finland, and Canada, each seeking to maximize the extent of its territorial borders in the Arctic. The contest is energized by global warming, which is opening up a new and shorter trade route between the Atlantic and the Pacific and exposing the region to new possibilities for commercial fishing and oil exploration. Not only does Professor Dodds insist that the outcome of this border-drawing contest is uncertain; he emphasizes that a neglected party greatly complicates matters insofar as it has long resisted and continues to resist the many, often violent impositions of sovereign state power on the region. He refers of course to the transnational Inuit people, who are demanding a large say in the reconfiguration of the North and are insisting that we think of the region in a way that is novel for sovereign states (cf. G7 Academies of Science, 2018).

Professor Emily Gilbert of the Canadian Studies Program and the Department of Geography and Planning at the University of Toronto next examines recent developments within, at, and away from the southern Canada-US border. She shows in detail how, since 9/11, border controls have been deepened and extended while the border itself has become more hardened to the mobility of some categories of people. Gilbert questions whether the investment is optimal. After all, nearly three-quarters of the 85 terrorist attacks resulting in fatalities on American soil between September 12, 2001, and December 31, 2016, were initiated by far right extremist groups, and 100 percent were "homegrown," involving no border crossings (United States Government Accountability Office 2017: 3-4). She also notes that legal, administrative and technological changes in surveillance, policing and border control have resulted in the erosion of Canadian sovereignty and the diminution of human rights. The latter is particularly evident among "irregular" refugees from Haiti, Ghana and elsewhere, and among people whose communities straddle the Canada-US border, such as the community of Derby Line (Vermont)/Stanstead (Quebec) and the Mohawk community of Akwesasne, which inhabits territory in Quebec, Ontario, and the state of New York. Members of these communities have resisted state control over, and disruptions of, their social and kinship ties, but to little avail. Gilbert concludes that resources are not being optimally directed, either from a security or a human rights perspective.

Finally, Heather Nicol of the Department of Geography at Trent University offers a critique of the preceding contributions. She seeks to demonstrate that the essays are insufficiently vocal concerning "the management of borders in the context of neoliberal restructuring and its consequences, the affective role of cyberspace in creating securitized spaces and discourses, the historical contextualization of bordering policies and strategies within continental structures of securitization in North America, and the relationship between borders and borderlands as sites of engagement and transformation." Said differently, Nicol reminds us that, within overarching global and continental constraints, the worm stubbornly turns while the doves persistently peck.

References

Brym, Robert, Melissa Godbout, Andreas Hoffbauer, Gabe Menard and Tony Zhang. 2014. "Social media in the 2011 Egyptian uprising." *British Journal of Sociology* 65(2): 266-92.

Brym, Robert, Anna Slavina, Mina Todosijevec and David Cowan. 2018. "Social movement horizontality in the Internet age? A critique of Castells in light of the Trump victory." Unpublished paper, Department of Sociology, University of Toronto.

Citizen Lab. 2017. "About the Citizen Lab." https://citizenlab.ca/about/.

Foucault, Michel. 1977 [1975]. *Discipline and Punish: The Birth of the Prison,* Alan Sheridan, trans. New York: Pantheon.

Foucault, Michel. 1981 [1976]. *The History of Sexuality: An Introduction,* vol. 1, Robert Hurley, trans. Harmondsworth, UK: Penguin.

G7 Academies of Science. 2018. The global arctic: the sustainability of communities in the context of changing ocean systems. https://www.leopoldina.org/uploads/tx_leopublication/2018_G7_Arctic_EN.pdf.

Google Maps. 2017. "Bir Tawil." https://www.google.ca/maps/@19.805 7024,36.7621017,6z.

Gordon, Neve. 2008. *Israel's Occupation.* Berkeley: University of California Press.

Hielord. 2015. "All countries that have ongoing territorial disputes with others." 8 August. http://brilliantmaps.com/territorial-disputes/.

Nance, Agnieszka B. 2008. "Introduction." Pp 1-8 in Agnieszka B. Nance, ed. *Literary and Cultural Images of a Nation without a State: The Case of Nineteenth Century Poland.* New York: Peter Lang.

Shakespeare, William. 1595. *The Third Part of King Henry the Sixth.* http://shakespeare.mit.edu/3henryvi/full.html.

United States Government Accountability Office. 2017. Countering Violent Extremism: Actions Needed to Define Strategy and Assess Progress of Federal Efforts. https://www.gao.gov/assets/690/683984.pdf.

Wells, H.G. 1920. *The Outline of History: Being a Plain History of Life and Mankind.* Garden City, NY: Garden City Publishing Co.

BORDERS AND BOUNDARIES

CHAPTER TWO
Bordered Futures in a Borderless World

John Hannigan

The Border Debate

Recently borders have assumed a high political profile across the world. Donald Trump's vow to erect a "beautiful wall" along the US-Mexico border, the Brexit vote and its aftermath, and contested borders in the Arctic and the South China Sea are just a few well known examples. At the 2017 Conservative Political Action Conference, influential alt-right ideologue and former chief presidential guru Steve Bannon described the "center core" of the Trump administration philosophy as "the belief that the United States is more than an economic unit in a borderless world. It is "a nation with a culture and a reason for being" (Caldwell 2017: 4). In *Fire and Fury*, Michael Wolff's (2018) explosive insider account of the Trump White House in its first year, Wolff writes, "Bannon believed that great numbers of people were suddenly receptive to a new message: the world needs borders—or the world should return to a time when it had borders."

People of a different ideological stripe find the whole idea of walls and national borders repugnant. As the award-winning Dutch journalist and historian Rutger Bregman (2017) argues, "borders are the single biggest cause of discrimination in all of world history. Inequality gaps between people living in the same country are nothing in comparison to those between separated global citizenries" (quoted in Foges 2018).

Boundaries too have become a focus of cultural conversations. A Google search for "crossing boundaries" yields 165 million hits, "breaking boundaries" more than 8 million, and "blurring boundaries" 2 million more. The blurring of boundaries (racial, sexual, religious, and so on) is a frequent movie theme. A Georgia O'Keefe painting entitled *Nature Forms—Gaspé* (1932), recently exhibited at the Art Gallery of Ontario, epitomizes the current vogue for boundary blurring (see http://bookerroseart.blogspot.ca/2013/09/georgia-okeeffe-abstraction.html). According to the curator's description:

Because she was born and bred in inland America, the ocean has a mesmerizing presence for her. With a focus on the turbulent water and rolling clouds, the image blurs the boundaries between figurative painting and abstraction, between land, sea and sky.

The distinction between borders and boundaries is itself frequently blurred. If not used interchangeably, the terms are often deployed in lockstep. The title of this this symposium is "The Future of Canada's Territorial Borders and Personal Boundaries," suggesting that the former is political, the latter personal. Another recent and useful take on this theme comes from anthropologist/sociologist Didier Fassin, the organizer of a 2015–16 workshop on "Borders and Boundaries" held at Princeton University's Institute for Advanced Studies. According to Fassin:

> The external limit of territories (borders) and the internal delimitations within societies (boundaries) have long been thought of in different terms: immigration, nationality and citizenship in the first case; racial, ethnic, religious, caste and class differentiation in the second. If globalization has hardened rather than abolished borders, it has also produced new realities and anxieties concerning social boundaries. *The immigrants of yesterday have become the minorities of today* (Fassin 2015; emphasis in the original).

Boundaries and borders have come to play a key role in contemporary conversations in the social sciences. Harvard sociologist Michèle Lamont observes that the idea of boundaries and its twin concept of borders "has been associated with research on cognition, social and collective identity, commensuration, census categories, cultural capital, cultural membership, racial and ethnic group positioning, hegemonic masculinity, professional jurisdictions, scientific controversies, group rights, immigration and contentious politics" (Lamont and Molnàr 2002: 167). More recently, Damon Mayrl and Sarah Quinn urge fellow sociologists to adequately theorize policy creation at the official edges of government. The "state-society-boundary," they argue, represents "one of the most fraught and consequential sites of boundary-making in contemporary life" (Mayrl and Quinn 2016: 1). This renewed interest stands in marked contrast to the 1970s and 1980s when the trend was to reject closed system or steady-state models in favour of open systems and organization-environment interaction featuring the porousness or fluidity of boundaries.

Canada has not been immune to the escalating debate over borders and boundaries. In a world perceived to be increasingly vulnerable to terrorist attack, the Canada-US border has been securitized through a series of controls and agreements. In Canada's North, the contest over maritime sovereignty has been intensifying. Individual boundaries are imperilled by heightened state surveillance and corporate tracking on the Internet. These issues are helping to shape the nature of Canadian identity, governmentality and security in Canada's 150th year as a sovereign nation.

Globalists vs. Territorialists

Broadly speaking, geopolitical discussions of borders and boundaries have pivoted on a debate between two "schools," globalists and territorialists. Globalists (not to be confused with the political and economic elite who are the *bête noire* of right-wing conspiracy theorists in the United States) anticipate the coming of a borderless world in which many boundaries have become more permeable to the flow of people, goods, capital and information, in no small part because of the reach of cyberspace (Westl-Walter 2010: 2). Twenty years ago, globalization scholarship was the flavour of the day. Globalization became linked to the "end of the nation-state" thesis. Many scholars asserted that political power was rapidly shifting away from the state toward free markets, multinational firms and global political associations such as the European Union (Community), NATO and the United Nations, all of which adopted policies that infringe on the sovereignty of the state (Newman 2003: 133).

According to an article in the *McKinsey Quarterly*, the ongoing digital revolution has accelerated recently with tremendous increases in electronic data, the ubiquity of mobile interfaces and the growing power of artificial intelligence. Together, these forces are provoking a reordering or redefinition of traditional industry borders and boundaries at a more rapid pace than we have previously experienced (Atluri et al. 2017).

Ron Deibert and his colleagues have been following the relationship between global connectivity, cyberspace security and political borders for decades. They have concluded that cyberspace is organized transnationally, not through the institutional structure of the state system; it has emergent properties that largely elude state control (Deibert and Rohozinski 2010: 15). This is not to say that we have reached the point of living in a completely borderless world.

With some success, governments monitor the Internet and impose varying degrees of censorship and control, creating new boundary forms. *Waxing borders,* such as semi-societal network organizations, allow restricted domestic Internet users to access international connections through offshore sites. *Virtual borders*, such as firewalls and encryption regimes, aim to stop unauthorized actors from viewing confidential information. In both cases, traditional state borders are eroded or removed (Deibert 2002).

The notion of a borderless world has long had considerable appeal for international humanitarian groups and scholars. *Médecins Sans Frontières* (Doctors without Borders) rose to prominence because they were the only medical relief group in Africa willing to carry out their activities across national borders, even in the face of opposition from national governments and rebel regimes. The Lampedusa Charter, a grassroots effort by North African and European activists to articulate a new set of rights for Mediterranean migrants, claims to be planetary in scope and urges readers to view Earth as a "shared space" (Ticktin 2016: 266).

Territorialists reply that the prospect of a globalized world has been overstated. They argue that rather than disappearing, boundaries are being extended and strengthened. The starting point for one of Heather Nicol's books is that "borders have continued relevance" and "'borderlessness' has not become the new basis of international organization in the late twentieth and early twenty-first centuries" (Nicol 2005: 214). In a similar key, Doris Wastl-Walter (2010: 2) points out that "the current world-wide political situation which is distinguished by the prevalence of fear of terrorism and security concerns can be interpreted as a sign for a 'reterritorialization' rather than a 'deterritorialization' of the world." And David Newman says that from a geographer's perspective, the "borderless world" argument is untenable:

> If there is anything that belies notions of a de-territorialized and borderless world more, it is the fact that boundaries in a variety of formats and intensities continue to demarcate the territories within which we interact and affiliate and the extent to which we are free to move from one space to another (Newman 2013: 123).

Borders are Everywhere
Much recent leading-edge scholarly work on bordered futures has been undertaken with the understanding that borders and their en-

forcement are far different today than they were in the past. Citing Balibar's (2004) notion that "borders are everywhere," Johnson and Jones (2011: 61) stress that borders should no longer be regarded simply as fixed lines on the political map of states. Rather, bordering work and practices that mark some bodies as legitimate and others as out of place occur far from the political border itself. In this reconceptualization, borders occur across a wide swath of everyday life. Cooper et al. (2014) have coined the concept of the "vernacularization of borders," by which they mean that the centre of gravity in border studies has begun to shift from a focus on nation-state borders to border work carried out by non-state actors in the realm of everyday experience. This shift offers "global connective possibilities" whereby "individuals are able to network across distant borders" (Wemyss 2017: 269).

Some researchers have observed that an increasing proportion of border security practices occur at considerable geographic distance from the actual political border and may be nearly or completely invisible. Airports have become major venues for sifting, sorting and excluding new arrivals to a country, yet they may be located hundreds of kilometres from the border itself. So too are railway terminals and maritime ports. Rumford (2011: 68) cites the case of the "juxtaposed" borders established by the UK along Eurostar train routes. The Container Security Initiative (CSI), launched in 2002 by the Bureau of Customs and Border Protection, posts American customs officials in foreign ports to inspect U.S.-bound cargo. It aims to "extend the zone of security outward so that American borders are the last line of defence, not the first" (Cowen 2010: 71). The 47 designated foreign CSI ports include Halifax, Montreal and Vancouver.

Rumford (2011: 68) says that borders can be "invisible," that is, "they are designed not to look like borders, located in one place but projected in another entirely." He cites as an example offshore borders such as those maintained by the EU Frontex boat patrols along the coast of West Africa. Such bordering activity, Rumford notes, is "designed to constitute a formidable physical barrier to those beyond the EU's border while not necessarily affecting those living on the inside." Alison Mountz has studied offshore border enforcement in detention centres on remote islands. Such islands, she says, "are part of a broader "enforcement archipelago" of detention, a tactic of migration patrol where legal ambiguity clouds migrants' status and spaces of asylum are shrunk (Mountz 2011: 126).

Furthermore, new technologies fundamentally transform the process of border security and enforcement, both at border check points and beyond. Johnson and Jones (2011: 61) cite as examples new border fences and biometric passports. In her interviews with "match analysts" at the UK's National Bordering Targeting Centre, Louise Amoore (2011: 64) found that the "spatial processes of searching and scanning, detention and deportation" are made by the application of security software that uses algorithmic risk models developed and written by mathematicians, software designers and computer scientists. An alert would flash on the computer screens of analysts and border guards if the profile of an airline passenger indicated some or all of the following: past travel to Pakistan, ticket paid in cash, ticket paid for by a third party, special meal request. Such "geo-graphing," Amoore notes, occurs "far away from the visible policing of the border line."

Another boundary-establishing activity that takes place far from formal lines on a map can be found in a very different arena—the geopolitics of deep oceans. The 1982 Law of the Sea Convention (LOSC), the first major revision to the maritime code in modern times, opened the door for a coastal nation to expand its claim to the subsurface rights over its portion of the continental shelf beyond the existing 200-mile nautical limit if it could prove scientifically that a geographical link exists between its land mass and adjacent underwater formations. The arbiter of this provision is a United Nations Agency, the Commission on the Limits of the Continental Shelf (CLCS). To date, the major arena for competition has been at the top of the world. Like the previous example of geo-graphing and computer-generated security alerts, this effort is a border-writing practice that draws legitimacy from a geo-scientific assessment, even as it is politically and economically motivated. Gone are the days when an intrepid explorer could plant a flag to claim absolute sovereignty over a territory. Much overheated media play was generated in 2007 when a Russian oceanographer placed a titanium flag at the bottom of the Arctic Ocean, beaming televised photos to the world, but the act had no legal standing. Boundary setting happens far away in scientific labs and government offices.

Several of the contributors to a 2011 state-of-the-art symposium in *Political Geography*, "Interventions on Rethinking 'The Border' in Border Studies," note that even as it has gained in breadth and sophistication, the theoretical landscape has occluded. Johnson and Jones note that as bordering practices become less the exclusive domain of the state and expand "well away from the border line itself to non-descript office parks and cyberspace," it becomes increasingly difficult to answer the "seemingly simple question of *who borders?*"

(Johnson and Jones 2011: 1-2, 62). Rumford (2011: 67-8) describes a "plethora of borders" that occupy a multiplicity of sites not just at the edges of the nation-state but diffused throughout society in towns and cities and local neighbourhoods. Examples include gated communities and CCTV surveillance. That bordering processes permeate everyday life is well-captured, he says, in John Urry's (2007) notion of the "frisk society." Recognizing that borders are woven into the fabric of society is a necessary step forward, Rumford argues, but it precludes coming up with straightforward answers to such questions as what constitutes a border, where can borders be found, and who is doing the bordering.

Borders, Boundaries and Borderlands

I want to briefly highlight an approach to border studies that offers exciting potential both for the field and for better understanding the future of Canadian society. In this view, it is imperative that we shift our scholarly gaze from borders to borderlands.

Borderlands are sometimes equated with "frontiers," defined as "the area in proximity to the border whose internal development was affected by the existence of this line" (Newman and Paasi 1998). However, this equivalency is flawed insofar as the term "frontier" summons up colonialist notions of geographically remote border states where lawlessness and dissent fester and order must be re-imposed. In keeping with the notion that "borders are everywhere," I suggest that the borderland is not limited to the state borderland but encompasses spaces in the centre (Horstmann 2002a).

The concept of borderlands is by no means new. *The Journal of Borderland Studies* was established in 1986. What is more recent is the notion of borderlands and their populations as possessing agency and identity apart from how they are framed by the state. Horstmann and Wodley (2006) draw a contrast between state borders, which are characterized by essentialized tradition and community, and borderlands, which are complex social systems. Rather than being dead zones, borderlands are vibrant sites of human agency. South (2017) describes borderlands as dynamic sites of social practice. Understanding them "not only deepens our appreciation of local social, economic, cultural and political processes but contributes towards a richer and de-centered analysis of national and international issues."

Social anthropologist Alexander Horstmann and his colleagues have explored this phenomenon empirically for over a decade in a series of case studies of networks of border people between Thailand, Malaysia and Myanmar who are mired in a "diasporic trap." On the one hand, they have been granted citizenship, albeit a special limited category of citizenship that withholds many state resources and certain rights. While they embrace a form of dual citizenship, defined partly by holding double identity cards, and partly through practice, life in these borderlands is anything but easy. For example, Thai fishers from Ben Sarai in southern Thailand fish illegally in Malaysian waters. If apprehended, they face the possibility of arrest and deportation. They are constantly at the mercy of unscrupulous brokers in border areas who benefit from their precarious status. Still, these trapped ethnic minorities find ways to liberate and empower their lives through border-crossing practices, notably strategies designed to build social ties with people in Malaysia, including village folk, kin, low-ranked police and middlemen in the fishing business with whom they forge patron-client relationships (Horstmann 2002b).

In similar fashion, Toronto sociologists Patricia Landolt and Luin Goldring have documented and analyzed the experience of a growing pool of refugees or those living in refugee-like situations in Canada. They argue that this proliferating population is marked by the experience of "precarious noncitizenship," which they describe as "a new fault line of social inequality in Canadian society." The relationship between noncitizenship, immobility, and inequality is evident in two overlapping areas of social life (Landolt 2017; Landolt and Goldring 2016). First, precarious noncitizenship is a crosscutting feature of the immigration system. Second, precarious noncitizenship mediates the relationship between immigration, work and labour markets.

Landolt and Goldring frame their studies of precarious noncitizenship within the perspectives of global migration and Canadian immigration policy. However, this approach might also be usefully explored in a broader discussion of borderlands and the vernacularization of borders. Like the border people of South Asia studied by Horstman and his co-researchers, the refugees studied by Landolt and Goldring are caught in a diasporic trap, possessing a fragile and temporary legal status that pivots on discretionary decisions by bureaucratic gatekeepers informed by narratives of deservingness and moral worthiness (Landolt 2017: 84). Looming always is the dreaded possibility of deportation.

What links these two cases is the necessity of reaching beyond what Miriam Ticktin (2016) calls "humanitarian borders." Ticktin argues that, as well-meaning as it is meant to be, humanitarianism at the border is not good enough. Charity or care is a form of welfare that is tied to the sovereignty of nation-states and includes the enforcement of borders. "If we want to change the situation at the borders of Europe and the United States," Ticktin insists, "we need another form of political care, one that reaches out beyond care as welfare in nation states, and beyond the benevolence of humanitarianism" (Ticktin 2016: 256). This revised form of political care must necessarily be anchored in legal and status rights that protect those who find themselves trapped in borderlands in situations of precariousness and vulnerability.

In a recently published book chapter, I focus on a less familiar example—victims of cross-border disasters (Hannigan 2018). Across the world, people displaced by typhoons, floods, tsunamis, earthquakes and other natural disasters regularly move back and forth across political borders. This phenomenon is likely to increase significantly in some regions as climate change accelerates and magnifies severe weather events. Environmental disaster migrants almost always lack fundamental legal status and protection in areas across the border where they flee. Norms may differ considerably from that of the home society. For example, cross-border female disaster victims may encounter difficulties where the host country is more patriarchal (Edwards 2009).

Noteworthy attempts to address this problem have been undertaken by the UN High Commission for Refugees and by the governments of Norway and Switzerland (the Nansen Initiative). If, after a prolonged period, return to one's country of origin proves impossible, permanent admission to the host country is recommended. Ideally, beneficiaries should be entitled to an array of status rights including access to the labour market, housing, health services, education, protection against discrimination and freedom of religion and opinion (Kalin and Schrepfer 2012). Ideally, of course, is the key word, and few, if any, governments have to date signed on to this initiative.

To borrow a phrase from David Harvey (2000), the challenge here is to transform borderlands from unsettled spaces of marginality and exclusion into emergent spaces of hope. In so doing, it is imperative to conceptualize the borderland both as a site of contestation and claims-making and as a laboratory of social change (Horstmann 2002a).

References

Amoore, L. 2011. "On the Line: Writing the Geography of the Virtual Border." *Political Geography* 30: 63-4.

Balibar, E. 2014. *We, the People of Europe? Reflections on Transnational Citizenship.* Princeton, NJ: Princeton University Press.

Bregman. R. 2017. *Utopia for Realists: How We Can Build the Ideal* World, translated by E. Manton. New York: Little Brown and Company.

Caldwell, C. 2017. "What Does Steve Bannon Want?" *The New York Times.* February 26, pp. 1, 4.

Cooper, A., Perkins, C. and C. Rumford. 2014. "The Vernacularization of Borders." Pp. 15-32 in *Placing the Border in Everyday Life,* edited by R. Jones and C. Johnson. London and New York: Routledge.

Cowen, D. 2010. "Containing Insecurity in US Port Cities and the 'War on Terror.'" Pp. 69-84 in *Disrupted Cities: When Infrastructure Fails,* edited by S. Graham. London: Routledge.

Deibert, R. 2002. "The Internet and the Borderless World." *ISUMA* 3(1). http://www.isuma.net/v03n01/deibert/deibert_e.shtml.

Deibert, R. and R. Rohozinski. 2010. "Risking Security: Policies and Paradoxes of Cyberspace Security." *International Political Sociology* 4(1): 15-32.

Edwards, F. 2009. "Effective Disaster Response in Cross-Border Events." *Journal of Contingencies and Crisis Management* 17 (4): 255-65.

Fassin, D. 2015. Borders and Boundaries. Princeton University, Institute of Advanced Study. https://www.sss.ias.edu/borders_and_boundaries.

Foges, C. 2018. "Our Turbulent World Needs Strong Walls." *The Times of London.* January 2.

Hannigan, J. 2018. "Disasters across Borders: Borderlands as Spaces of Hope and Innovation in the Geopolitics of Environmental Disasters." Pp. 79-96 in *Crossing Borders; Governing Environmental Disasters in a Global Age in Asia and the Pacific,* edited by M. Miller, M. Douglass and M. Garschagen. Singapore: Springer.

Horstmann, A. 2002. "Incorporation and Resistance: Border Crossings and Social Transformation in Southeast Asia." *Anthropologi Indonesia* 67: 12-29.

Horstmann, A. 2002b. *Dual Ethnic Minorities and the Local Reworking of Citizenship at the Thailand-Malaysian Border.* CIBR Working Papers in Border Studies, no. CIBR/WP02-3. https://www.qub.ac.uk/research-centres/CentreforInternationalBordersResearch/Publications/WorkingPapers/CIBRWorkingPapers/Filetoupload,174412,en.pdf.

Horstmann, A. and R. Wadley. 2006. "Introduction." Pp. 1-26 in *Covering the Margin: Agency and Narrative in Asian Borderlands,* edited by A. Horstmann and R. Wadley. New York: Bergdahn Books.

Johnson, C. and R. Jones. 2011. "Rethinking 'the border' in border studies." *Political Geography* 30: 61-2.

Kalin, W. and N. Schrepfer. 2012. *Protecting People Crossing Borders in the Context of Climate Change: Normative Gaps and Possible Approaches.*

Geneva: United Nations High Commission for Refugees. http://www. unher.org/protect.

Lamont, M. and V. Molnár. 2002. "The Study of Boundaries in the Social Sciences." *Annual Review of Sociology* 28: 167-95.

Landolt, P. 2017. "Immigration, Precarious Noncitizenship, and the Changing Landscape of Work." Pp. 81-104 in *Immigration and the Future of Canadian Society: Proceedings of the Second S.D. Clark Symposium on the Future of Canadian Society*, edited by R. Brym. Oakville, ON: Rock's Mills Press.

Landolt, P. and L. Goldring. 2016. "Assembling Noncitizenship through the Work of Conditionality." *Citizenship Studies* 19(8): 853-69.

Mayrl, D. and S. Quinn. 2016. "Defining the State from Within: Boundaries, Schemas and Associational Policymaking." *Sociological Theory* 34(1): 1-26.

Mountz, A. 2011. "The Enforcement Archipelago: Detention, Haunting, and Asylum on Islands." *Political Geography* 30: 118-28.

Newman, D. 2013. "Boundaries." Pp.123-37 in *A Companion to Political Geography*, edited by J. Agnew, K. Mitchell and G. Toal (Ó'Tuathail). Malden, MA: Blackwell.

Nicol, H. 2005. "Conclusion." Pp. 414-19 in *Holding the Line: Borders in a Global World*, edited by H. Nicol and I. Townsend. Vancouver: UBC Press.

Rumford, C. 2011. "Seeing Like a Border." *Political Geography* 30: 67-9.

South, A. 2017. Review of S. Oh (ed.), *Mynamar's Mountain and Maritime Borderscapes: Local Practices, Boundary-making and Figured Worlds*. Singapore: Institute of Southeast Asia Studies, 2016. *Journal of Contemporary Asia* 47 (4): 674-6.

Ticktin, M. 2016. "Thinking Beyond Humanitarian Borders." *Social Research* 83(2): 255-71.

Urry, J. 2007. *Mobilities*. Oxford: Polity Press.

Wastl-Walter, D. 2010. "Introduction." Pp. 1-8 in *The Ashgate Research Companion to Border Studies*, edited by D. Wastl-Walter. Surrey: Ashgate.

Wemyss, G. 2017. Review of R. Jones and C. Johnson (eds.), *Placing the Border in Everyday Life*, London and New York: Routledge, 2014. *Journal of Borderland Studies* 32 (2): 269-70.

Wolff, M. 2018. *Fire and Fury: Inside the Trump White House*. New York: Henry Holt and Co.

CHAPTER THREE

Boundaries and Borders in Global Cyberspace[1]

Ronald J. Deibert and Louis W. Pauly

Introduction

As the Internet developed and spread in popularity in the 1990s and early 2000s, many observers predicted it would present a major challenge to the sovereign authority of states in general and to the control capabilities of authoritarian states in particular (Johnson and Post 1996). Some went so far as to forecast a borderless digital world or even the dissolution of organized government and the states system altogether. More recent research and commentary has emphasized the opposite: the expansion and intensification of controls over cyberspace by states within conventional territorial boundaries. As Demchak and Dombrowski (2011; 35) put it, "from India to Sweden, nations are demanding control over what happens electronically in their territory, even if it is to or from the computers of their citizens."

While policy efforts to re-territorialize cyberspace are undeniable, growing concern about them has obscured the extent to which states simultaneously project power in and through global cyberspace outside of their territorial jurisdictions. Expanding state involvement in cyberspace does not stop at the border; extraterritorial projections of state power through cyberspace are expanding, deepening and becoming more elaborate. Not surprisingly, the most extensive of these projections come from the United States, but even the most autocratic regimes associated with efforts to promote "Internet sovereignty" or "cyberautarky" increasingly project cyberpower outside their territorial boundaries.

States are exercising extraterritorial prerogatives to acquire data about the world around them: to anticipate, analyze and interdict threats; to shape the systemic environment to their strategic advantage; to support other forms of material power that are also being

---

1. Portions of this paper are derived from Ronald J. Deibert and Louis W. Pauly, "Cyber Westphalia and Beyond: Extraterritoriality and Mutual Entanglement in Cyberspace," paper presented at the annual meeting of the International Studies Association, Baltimore, February 2017.

reconstituted globally via the movement of goods and services, production and transportation systems. Through traditional as well as mercenary armed forces and proxy groups, they are also using new communication technologies to broaden command and control systems and to defend and promote a broad set of strategic interests. The combined if unintended "network effect" of states engaging in such extraterritorial projections of power through cyberspace is to frustrate individual state strategies aimed at territorial insulation.

This paper begins by summarizing evidence for territorialization in cyberspace. We then turn to several case studies of extraterritorial projections of power, beginning with the "easy case" of the United States followed by several examples from authoritarian regimes.

Territorialization in Cyberspace

A useful way to conceptualize growing state controls over cyberspace within territorial boundaries is the framework developed as part of the OpenNet Initiative (ONI) that defines several generations of information controls (Deibert 2015; Deibert and Rohozinski 2008).

First-generation controls refer to basic Internet censorship systems erected at national borders, with governments restricting their citizens' access to online content beyond—the Great Firewall of China being the archetypal example. At one point in the late 2000s, ONI tested for national-level Internet filtering in more than 70 countries and found evidence in more than 45 (Deibert, Palfrey, Rohozinski, and Zittrain 2008; 2010; 2012). The number is probably considerably higher now, and includes many liberal-democratic countries that censor Internet content involving the sexual exploitation of children, hate speech or "terrorist"-related content.

Second-generation controls refer to government measures to control cyberspace domestically through laws, policies and other sorts of policing of the Internet, often undertaken with the cooperation of private companies. Examples of second-generation controls include content removal requests, legal or other types of compelled access to customer data (e.g, through surveillance systems or "back doors"), and the application of defamation or libel laws to Internet content. Sometimes second-generation controls are applied informally or secretly, especially around national security measures, making documentation challenging for researchers.

Occasionally we see glimpses of these controls through the window of private sector transparency reports, such as those published by Google, Microsoft, Twitter or the remarkable Vodafone Law Enforcement Disclosure Report (Vodafone 2014), published in 2014, that extensively documented country-by-country requests for Vodafone's customer data.

There are other ways to catch glimpses of these controls. Citizen Lab has employed reverse engineering methods to uncover hidden surveillance or censorship functions built inside popular applications, such as the surveillance embedded inside the Chinese version of Skype, or the collection of sensitive user information in popular mobile browser applications manufactured by Baidu, UC, WeChat, and QQ (about which more will be said below) (Dalek et al. 2015; Knockel, McKune, and Senft 2016; Knockel, Senft, and Deibert 2016; Villeneuve 2008). It is accurate to say that second-generation controls are becoming more complex, penetrating deeper into societies and reigning in the once free-flowing environment of the Internet with a thicket of formal and informal rules, laws and practices.

Third-generation controls refer to the use by states of more "offensive" information methods, such as targeted surveillance and digital attack techniques. If first-generation controls refer to building borders, and second-generation controls to deepening those controls into domestic politics, third-generation controls are about projecting outwards and going on the offense. Many governments' armed forces and intelligence agencies have developed cyberattack capabilities, varying in resources and capabilities. Growing demands for offensive cyber capabilities have produced a massive market for cyber war and surveillance products and services developed by private companies, ranging from Cold War giants like Raytheon and Northrop Grumman to more obscure "niche" companies, like Italy's Hacking Team, the UK's Gamma Group and the Israeli "cyber warfare" company, NSO Group (Harris 2014). The cyber security industry is growing at an annual rate of 24 percent per year, and it is estimated that it will be worth over USD $600bn annually by 2023 (Stiennon 2016). Citizen Lab has documented an extensive proliferation of mass surveillance and targeted commercial spyware products and services to numerous countries worldwide, many of them autocratic or repressive regimes who use them to control dissent (about which more will be said below).

A major impetus for all three generations of information controls has been the growing incentive governments face to secure cyberspace. Cyber security is now widely recognized as being at the top of the policy agenda for most countries, driven by repeated instances of large-scale data breaches and vulnerabilities to critical infrastructure, as well as concerns around an "arms" race in cyberspace, which leads to competitive behavior among state adversaries. Of course, the meaning of "cyber security" varies widely from country to country and is inherently political, however much it may be construed as a technical exercise. For some, cyber security is primarily about shoring up critical infrastructure and dealing with public-private cooperation problems regardless of political boundaries. For many others, however, cyber security translates into control of domestic opposition, social movements, illicit networks or mass surveillance of entire populations under the rubric of counterterrorism (Deibert and Rohozinski 2010).

To the three generations of controls might be added a fourth: the efforts by some states to legitimize territorial controls over the Internet through governance agreements at regional and international levels. Over the last several years, a coalition of like-minded countries, led by China and Russia, has spearheaded a movement to adjust Internet governance away from what they perceive as its current US-dominated system to one that is centred more around the United Nations system and organizations like the International Telecommunications Union, and which recognizes "Internet sovereignty" as a bedrock principle (Deibert and Crete-Nishihata 2012). The coalition's agenda is attractive to many countries, particularly after the Edward Snowden disclosures. It has nevertheless been met with much hand-wringing by Internet freedom advocates, businesses, civil society and western policymakers.

Expanding state controls over cyberspace have indeed been widely noted. It is now commonplace to hear about territorializing pressures on the Internet, which has led to predictions of a coming Internet "fragmentation" or "Cyber Westphalia" (Dombrowski 2016; Demchak and Dombrowski, 2011).[2] A major report published in January 2016 for the World Economic Forum summarizes and evaluates many of these viewpoints (Drake, Cerf and Kleinwächter 2016). The report highlights ten different types of government-based Internet fragmentation trends, including filtering and blocking websites, social networks or other resources offering undesired contents; attacks on information resources offering undesired contents; digital protectionism blocking users' access to and use of key platforms and tools for electronic commerce; centralizing and terminating international interconnection; attacks on national networks and key assets; local data processing and/or retention requirements; architectural or routing changes to keep data flows within a territory; prohibitions

2. The 1648 Treaty of Westphalia ending the Thirty Years War established the norm of states not interfering in the affairs of other states.

on the transborder movement of certain categories of data; strategies to construct "national Internet segments" or "cyber-sovereignty;" and international frameworks intended to legitimize restrictive practices.

Of these, one of the more important measures is the so-called "data localization" trend, accelerated by reaction to the Edward Snowden disclosures. Many western and non-western countries have reacted to revelations of spying by the United States' NSA and its signals intelligence (SIGINT) partners in the "Five Eyes" alliance by pushing for new requirements that would restrict hosting of data to local jurisdictions and domestic companies or restrict transborder processing of certain classes of data. The most prominent of these data localization efforts has been the German "Schengen Cloud" routing proposal put forward by Deutsche Telekom and others within German industry and government. Brazil, China, Russia, Indonesia and many other countries have promoted similar data localization requirements.

While the explicit rationale behind these efforts assumes that data localization will ostensibly protect against Five Eye surveillance (a highly questionable assumption), some policymakers and others have raised concerns that the efforts are an excuse for the exercise of growing state controls. It is much easier to compel local companies to turn over data to law enforcement when it is stored in domestic jurisdictions as opposed to making requests to foreign companies through cumbersome mutual legal assistance treaties (MLAT) or other international processes that can take months or years. Taken to their logical conclusion, efforts to enforce data localization, alongside other trends in state control, would have the combined effect of fragmenting the Internet.

However striking these impulses toward re-territorialization may seem, it is important not to overstate their implications. They constitute only one dimension of a complex process. Growing state-led information controls cannot accurately be described as a simple re-imposition of Westphalian principles over cyberspace. Nor will they necessarily mean the breakup or fragmentation of the Internet. These trends are countered by the complex effects of the extraterritorial projection of state power into cyberspace itself. The next section surveys several cases to illustrate the dynamic tension now reshaping cyberspace and the ways that authorities are trying to exploit and regulate it.

Extraterritoriality in Cyberspace

THE UNITED STATES

The American defense of a borderless, open Internet may be depicted as based entirely on liberal values and ideals, and conveniently contrasted with the "territorializing" processes of states that oppose this agenda. The US posture is actually more complicated. Its "Internet freedom" agenda is arguably more a function of interests than values. It is in many ways a discursive or ideological support for the projection of US power globally. In this respect, it is analogous to the US position on treating the oceans and outer space as a "commons"—free movement of information globally (like free navigation of navies, satellites and, to a lesser degree, aircraft) serves global hegemonic power, not because US policymakers believe in the ideal of the open commons (although some might) but because sustaining their position of predominance depends on the ability to move goods, services, information and capabilities globally.

The need to project power globally is also connected to a changing threat environment. The US threat perspective is now truly global in scope: threats are anywhere, anytime, everywhere. Its extended, worldwide interests necessitate a globally distributed diplomatic, military and intelligence footprint. To wit, consider that the US now operates nearly 800 military bases in more than 70 countries and territories (Vine 2015). This extended footprint is woven together by a bristling network of digital communications. The US currently has 131 government satellites and 149 military satellites in orbit. Another 273 US-owned commercial satellites add to the mix (Union of Concerned Scientists 2016). The Pentagon alone operates around 7,000 unmanned aerial drones (Friends Committee on National Legislation 2015). A targeted Hellfire missile strike from any Predator drone, such as those that occur frequently in Pakistan or Yemen, is guided by earth-orbiting global positioning satellites (GPS) to within a few metres of its target and is typically fired by an operator in a hangar in Nevada, eyes fixed on computer screens onto which are projected high-resolution images beamed back instantly from the Predator's advanced imaging sensors. While the United States is, according to international legal principles, a sovereign state just like any other, in practice it is radically unlike any other state. The exercise of its power, driven by a worldwide perception of national interest, is projected materially around the entire planet.

It is also important to put the US position into historical perspective. The development of the Internet, and the technologies that preceded it and from which it arose (such as the telegraph, telecommunications and earth orbiting satellites and the digital computing systems that instruct them) were inextricably bound up with the emergence of the United States as a global superpower. From the first undersea cables to telecommunications networks to satellites and now thousands of drones feeding data back to control systems and databases, these technologies underpin a highly integrated and wired armed forces and intelligence system that is planetary in scope. Globalization, the Internet, and US power are thus part of a single historical system. Because of that historical starting point, the United States enjoys a distinct "home field advantage" with respect to much of the geopolitics of cyberspace. Most of the Tier 1 telecommunications companies that operate the backbone of the earth's communications systems are headquartered in the United States. Most of the largest software, social media, device and Internet services companies—Microsoft, Google, Apple, Facebook, Amazon— are American (Deibert 2012).

It is true that companies can be coerced, legally compelled, and otherwise enrolled in US government policing and intelligence efforts precisely because they are US owned and operated—a lesson not lost on challengers and adversaries, as illustrated in data localization efforts described earlier. Nevertheless, this does not mean they will always comply, as the FBI/Apple case illustrates. Indeed, one of the more interesting consequences of the Snowden disclosures has been the rolling out of consumer-level end-to-end encryption and a greater unwillingness on the part of the US-based private sector to bend to law enforcement and other government agency demands. This new independent posture on the part of IT companies, while obviously self-serving in the short run, appears likely to deepen and extend global networks and continue to frustrate state efforts around data localization and territorialization.

This intentional extraterritorial projection of US governmental power is reflected most clearly (but also obscurely because of its highly classified nature) in the realm of SIGINT. US SIGINT capabilities match the United States' globally-scaled interests. They are dependent on a projection of US intelligence agencies' reach into networks physically based outside the territorial jurisdiction of the United States proper. This reach is facilitated in a number of ways: through the assistance of US telecommunications and software companies that act as a "proxy" and are compelled by legal instruments, classified or otherwise. The reach is also enabled by the position of collection points at key junctures along the global information infrastructure outside of the territorial jurisdiction of the United States (satellites, drones, aerial SIGINT, undersea cable tapping, etc.). It is also undertaken by remote access to servers, routers and Internet Exchange Points (IXPs) that are critical "chokepoints" in the flow of global communications. The latter can happen in a number of ways: from targeted attacks on individuals whose compromise would allow access to those chokepoints (e.g., system administrators at IXPs); by exploitation of vulnerabilities in code that can be exploited remotely; by clandestinely propagating weaknesses in encryption standards through international standard-setting bodies (e.g., the Dual EC DRBG standard); and by deliberating tampering with hardware and switches that are then shipped overseas.

The reasons for this type of extraterritorial reach should be obvious but are sometimes overlooked. Power depends on having access to information that can be utilized as data for intelligence and decision making, but the data must be sourced globally given the globally interconnected nature of today's world economy, the nature of the distributed threat environment (ISIS, Al Qaeda), questions of access to critical resources, monitoring of adversaries' intentions and other factors. It must then be communicated back to decision makers. The global threat environment necessitates globally networked power projection and intelligence gathering capabilities.

International relations inscribes an age-old story of the diffusion of practices and the emulation of norms. Just as the leading states go, so it is reasonable to infer that other countries will follow. Of course, the tempo, reach and dimensions of the extraterritorial projection of cyber power may vary depending on the country in question. Its specific manifestations are a function of many factors, including region, ethnicity, culture, organizational norms, threat perceptions and other regime idiosyncrasies. Below, we highlight several "hard" country cases where we can see compelling evidence of the extraterritorial projection of state power in cyberspace among those states most often associated with the idea of re-territorialization, or Cyber Westphalia.

China is the paradigmatic country for Internet territorialization. It employs all three generations of information controls, from its Great Firewall that blocks access to websites hosted outside of China's borders, to its extensive, legally mandated system of social media controls imposed on domestic Internet service companies and providers. Companies employ thousands of individuals whose job is to censor posts on popular social media and other communications platforms. Many engineer their systems with surveillance functionalities and all companies are required to share user data with state security services on request. Internationally, China leads an effort to bolster normative support among like-minded countries for an Internet governance regime in which state sovereignty is prioritized.

Despite its continuing efforts to guard its cyber borders, China is also well known for its extraterritorial applications of state power. Such practices are most evident in vast and well documented cyber espionage campaigns, which include global targets and an extensive transnational network of command and control servers based outside of China's jurisdiction. Apart from its extraterritorial projection of power through cyber espionage campaigns, China also has extensive transnational reach through its IT, telecom and software industry. China's Huawei is the largest telecommunications equipment manufacturer in the world.

At the same time that Chinese authorities vigorously defend their Internet border, they also are pragmatic about the need to tend to transnational data flows, principally for economic reasons (Lindsay 2015a). The Great Firewall of China is porous, not by accident or poor design, but by intention. To cite just one example, CloudFlare, a US-based cyber-security firm, recently entered into a "virtual joint venture" with Chinese web-services firm Baidu to create a unified network that makes foreign websites more easily accessible in China and allows Chinese sites to run in destinations outside the country (Mozur 2015). While the agreement may seem orthogonal to the regime's interest in strictly defending its territorial boundaries, it is perfectly congruent with the pragmatic approach the country's elites take with respect to encouraging economic growth and the digital networks that are essential to that growth, while maintaining a lid on the exchange of ideas that run contrary to one-party rule or that touch on taboo topics, such as religious freedom, democracy and human rights.

Another vivid illustration of China's extraterritorial projection of power into cyberspace is its ambitious, though byzantine and secretive, national space program. China now has 177 satellites in orbit, second only to the United States (568) and surpassing Russia (133). These satellites include those whose purpose is communications, navigation, civil defence, remote sensing and surveillance, as well as science and environmental monitoring. China also has a manned space program and has ambitions to land a man on the moon by 2023. One of the cornerstones of China's space program is its commercial launch offering. China has launched satellites for numerous countries and companies. Its Long March (Chang Zheng) family of rockets is responsible for 155 satellites currently in orbit, second only to the Ariane family operated by a European consortium of countries (which is responsible for 200). This market is important to China for both revenue and national prestige, and shows China's commitment to extraterritorial projections of power in cyberspace. That a country described by many as the archetype of Cyber Westphalia is also one of the world's leading purveyors of systemic Earth monitoring should indicate that the simple "territorialization" paradigm requires conceptual adjustment.

IRAN

Iran is also held up as a prime example of Internet fragmentation. It has one of the most extensive national Internet filtering systems, and its controls embody all three generations outlined earlier. In recent years, the country has created several new agencies to oversee information controls, including the Supreme Council of Cyberspace, the Cyber Army, the Committee Charged with Determining the Instances of Offensive Content, and the Cyber Defense Command. Iran has been developing plans and gradually rolling out technology for a national Intranet walled off from the global Internet, called the "Internet E-Paak" or "clean Internet." It routinely throttles bandwidth to slow down connections to virtual private networks and circumvention tools around major events, like elections (ASL19 and Psiphon 2013; Citizen Lab and ASL19 2013; Small Media 2015). Iran has even collaborated with China, and Chinese companies, on its domestic information controls regime. China's ZTE reportedly sold Iranian telecommunications carriers sophisticated equipment capable of monitoring backbone-level communications and intercepting emails, SMS and telephone calls (Stecklow 2012).

Yet Iran also employs a fairly advanced cyber espionage capability that is used to target state adversaries and to gather information on dissidents and human rights activists in the global diaspora. One of the cyber espionage campaigns attributed to the Iranian government, called Newscaster, exploited several Internet and social media services to target "senior U.S. military and diplomatic personnel, congressional personnel, Washington D.C. area journalists, U.S. think tanks, defense contractors in the U.S. and Israel, as well as others who are vocal supporters of Israel" (Ward 2014). Newscaster worked by creating fake social media accounts, friending and linking to targets, and then sending spear phishing emails containing documents embedded with, or links to, malicious software, which were then used to harvest email and other log-in credentials of victims. A 2015 Citizen Lab report documented a similar Iranian-based spear phishing campaign that attempted to trick users into giving up their credentials to Gmail accounts, even bypassing Google's two-factor authentication security measures in the process (Scott-Railton and Kleemola 2015).

In these and other Iranian cyber espionage campaigns, Iranian state agencies or their proxies maneuver through global cyberspace to operate internationally, gather information on adversaries' intentions and neutralize opposition based abroad. The actions of Iran in cyberspace can thus be seen as a continuation of what Iran has been doing in more conventional terms for many years. Although details are lacking, as part of longstanding clandestine intelligence support to the Assad regime in Syria it is possible Iran has assisted in the organization of targeted digital attacks on the Syrian opposition (Regalado, Villeneuve, and Scott-Railton 2015). Alongside the flow of finances, weapons and strategic intelligence to Hezbollah, Iranian intelligence may have also supplied eavesdropping and other information warfare technology leading up to and during the 2006 summer war with Israel (Cordesman, Sullivan and Sullivan 2007; Wege 2012). After the US- and Israeli-organized Stuxnet attack on its nuclear centrifuges, Iran may have repurposed the same malware to target the computers of rival Saudi Arabia's Aramco refineries (Zetter 2014). To depict Iran as a model of Cyber Westphalia obscures the extent to which Iran, like many other countries, has an elaborate outward-facing and internationally-engaging cyber strategy that goes beyond Iranian territorial space and which is a digital continuation of its longstanding power projection activities.

Much like China, the Iranian regime faces the classic "dictator's dilemma" concerning Internet controls: as much as it wants to limit and contain the free flow of information, it depends on transborder communications for a myriad of commercial exchanges (Howard, Agarwal, and Hussain 2011). Consider the practical trade-offs facing Iran in their efforts to throttle access to certain VPNs used to circumvent Iranian firewalls. Traditionally, throttling circumvention tools has come at a price; connections to banking and other financial services using the same encryption protocols have been disrupted, much to the chagrin of Iranian businesses and elites. Recently, Citizen Lab researchers have observed Iranian information controls becoming much more fine-grained and precise, targeting the specific protocols associated with popular VPNs while limiting collateral damage to https connections associated with financial exchanges. This evolution of information controls shows both a maturation of techniques but also clear evidence of the importance of transborder traffic to the Iranian economy. As much as Iranian rhetoric may suggest a desire to wall themselves off entirely from global cyberspace (rhetoric picked up on and repeated by concerned observers in the West), actual Iranian practices suggest a much more nuanced balancing act and a fairly robust international engagement in cyberspace for both benign and malicious reasons.

Russia

Under Vladimir Putin, Russia has gradually reverted to authoritarian rule, part of which includes a tightening grip on information controls in Russian cyberspace. A major impetus behind these controls was the 2011 anti-government protests, organized through social media, which took Russian authorities by surprise. To contain future demonstrations of this sort, Russian authorities ramped up pressure on Internet companies to conform to Russian government policies. Today, Russia evinces all of the elements of Cyber Westphalia—sweeping data localization laws imposed on foreign Internet giants like Facebook, Google, Twitter and Linkedin, a broadening Internet censorship regime, arrests and intimidation of independent media and bloggers and an architecture of wholesale mass surveillance undertaken by the installation of equipment at telecommunications companies, known as the SORM system (Soldatov and Borogan 2015). Russia and China have even cooperated around information controls; in April 2016, Russia hosted the first Russia-China cyber security forum to share strategies and best practices. The meeting included Lu Wei, head of China's State Internet Information Office and Fang Bixang, the man widely thought to be the "father" of China's Great Firewall.

As in China, Russia's information controls are not limited by its territorial boundaries. Russia's approach to cyberspace is highly elaborated. It is a key part of a larger information "warfare" strategy that includes industrial-scale cyber espionage and targeted digital attacks, sophisticated propaganda and disinformation campaigns through state controlled media organs and the extension of Russian equipment, technology and know-how to former client states, particularly in the former Soviet republics. For example, all of the Commonwealth of Independent States have in place a SORM-compliant system of mass surveillance, the technical equipment for which is shared by Russian security services. Russian manufactured telecommunications routers are deployed throughout Asia, and may contain hidden surveillance functions engineered to allow Russian interception. CIS countries coordinate their cyber security strategies through regional forums like the Shanghai Cooperation Organization (the SCO), which also includes China, Iran and Pakistan. The SCO has strategized collectively on how to repel social media inspired protests, which are typically framed in the rubric of "counter terrorism."

Like the US and China, Russia is widely considered to be a tier-one cyber espionage power connected to many international cyber espionage campaigns. It is widely assumed Russian SIGINT makes use of the talented organized criminal groups that have long flourished in Russia and whose skills are connected to the thriving science, technology, engineering and mathematics programs in the country. The use of organized crime for offensive cyber operations is a convenient way to reap the benefits of such attacks while providing for plausible deniability, as evidenced in Estonia in 2007, Georgia in 2008 (Deibert, Rohozinski and Crete-Nishihata 2012), and more recently in the Ukraine (about which more will be said below). Russian SIGINT campaigns show extraordinary skill at leveraging a multitude of mostly free Internet services to reach far across global cyberspace to gather information. Consider the so-called "Turla Group" cyber espionage campaign, which affected many high-value targets in dozens of countries worldwide and which uses satellite uplinks as command and control servers (Tanase 2015). Another sophisticated Russian cyber espionage campaign, FireEye 2015, referred to in the security industry as APT29, uses a digital mélange of Internet tools such as Twitter, Github, filesharing and cloud computing services to globally distribute its command-and-control infrastructure and help obfuscate the origins of its cyber espionage campaign (Lennon 2015).

One of the distinct traits of Russian cyber espionage are its "influence operations," which have a long history connecting back to the Soviet period and are digital variations of Cold War propaganda, disinformation and other espionage campaigns. For example, Russia makes extensive use of social media to discredit and sow discord among adversaries, including the use of paid "trolls" who post messages favourable to the Putin regime or harass those who oppose it. Its long-standing use of "Kompromat"—"compromising material" used to discredit political opponents with embarrassing information typically acquired clandestinely—was taken to a new level with the intrusions into the email networks of prominent Democratic Party officials in 2016. Information acquired by Russian-backed cyber espionage actors was provided to Wikileaks and other social media, ostensibly to discredit Hillary Clinton. While Russia promotes territorially-based information controls in international spheres and routinely censors social media, its digital influence operations show that it also actively engages social media abroad for its power projection aims, however illicit these may be.

Russia's incursions into Ukraine, including its annexation of Crimea in March 2014, illustrate well both the extraterritorial projection of cyber power and its limitations. Thanks to overlapping telecommunications companies, infrastructure, shared engineering assets and common technical protocols that derive from a common starting point, Russia has historically enjoyed dominance over Ukrainian cyberspace. This dominance meant that Russia could easily maneuver through Ukrainian cyberspace at will, monitor activities and mount targeted but isolated malware attacks meant to confuse, weaken and compromise adversaries. At the same time, Russia had no incentive to disrupt Ukrainian cyberspace entirely. Even the December 2015 attack on Ukraine's power grid, which caused a massive power outage lasting several days and affected a quarter of a million Ukrainians, and which was widely attributed to Russian-based hackers who reportedly undertook months of preparation and reconnaissance, was limited in scope and scale.

Perhaps the countries one would least likely expect to project power extraterritorially would be lower-tier authoritarian, mixed or hybrid regimes and countries like those in the Persian Gulf, sub-Saharan Africa, the Middle East and North Africa, Asia, Latin America and the countries of the former Soviet Union other than Russia. Countries like Saudi Arabia, the UAE, Bahrain, Sudan, Ethiopia, Egypt, Syria, Vietnam, Thailand, Singapore, Pakistan, Myanmar, Venezuela, Uzbekistan, Tajikistan, Kyrgyzstan and Kazakhstan are, arguably, principal examples of a coming Cyber Westphalia. Countries such as these have all moved aggressively to control domestic information space through technical and regulatory means, and in every case listed above have Internet censorship systems in place to block access to information that crosses their territorial borders. These countries are also considered principal supporters of Russian and Chinese-backed international initiatives on "Internet sovereignty," and many of them have introduced data localization regulations.

Yet, as Citizen Lab research has shown, all of these countries have also adopted third-generation offensive control techniques that include the projection of state power beyond territorial boundaries. One example of this tendency is the use of commercial spyware. Many of the countries listed above have been documented purchasing sophisticated commercial spyware and surveillance technologies from western vendors like the UK's Finfisher and Italy's Hacking Team. As Citizen Lab research has shown in detail, those systems involve complicated transnational infrastructures, and include the targeting of groups and individuals in remote regions of the world (Marczak, Guarnieri, Marquis-Boire, and Scott-Railton 2014a; 2014b; Marczak, Scott-Railton, and McKune 2015; Marczak et al. 2014;2015; Marquis-Boire 2012a; 2012b; 2014; Marquis-Boire, Marczak, and Guarnieri 2012; Marquis-Boire, Marczak, Guarnieri, and Scott-Railton 2013a;2013b; Marquis-Boire, Scott-Railton, Guarnieri, and Kleemola 2014; see Figure 3.1 and Figure 3.2).

For purposes of our discussion, what is remarkable about both of these cases is that many of the targets and victims are located outside of the client countries, and typically involve human rights organizations, journalists, and other regime critics within the global diaspora. For example, the government of Ethiopia has employed Hacking Team spyware and Finfisher products to target journalists in the United Kingdom and the United States. Figure 3.3 illustrates the foreign espionage infrastructure operating in the United States using Hacking Team software.

The other interesting aspect of these services is that they work by exploiting global hosting and network services to obfuscate the origins of the attacks and mask the country clients from their victims. Figure 3.4 illustrates the transnational networks used by Mexican and Moroccan espionage campaigns operating with Hacking Team software.

Conclusion

The picture emerging from the research outlined above complicates the narrative of a coming Cyber Westphalia. While it is true that there are growing government controls over cyberspace within territorial boundaries, these trends need to be balanced against the insistent and expanding extraterritorial projection of power in and through cyberspace by even the most autocratic regimes. US hegemony in cyberspace is an historical artefact. Its legacy is now being contested by competing European, Chinese and Indian manufacturers and users of a global telecommunications infrastructure. The more all of these countries depend on external markets for revenue, material support and intelligence collection, the more they have a stake in the persistence of a cyberspace infrastructure that, while politicised in various ways, remains "open" at a fundamental level. Even second- and third-tier powers are beginning to exploit that openness, albeit at lower levels of capacity and intensity.

The combined effects of extraterritorial projections of power contribute to a deepening mutual entanglement that may well act as a deterrent to overt cyber warfare and a constraint on otherwise catastrophic cyberattacks. All states now depend on and benefit from global networks, and even the most autocratic have reasons not to disable or destroy them entirely. They depend on them for intelligence. They depend on them for commerce, whether in legal, grey or black markets. Their elites depend on them for finance, investment, information and protection. What is commonly labelled "the offshore world" could not exist today in the absence of such networks. Despite all the attention recently paid to issues of money laundering, tax evasion and tax avoidance, little evidence exists of a transnational consensus on moving to close down that world. And the reasons are not simply commercial, financial or attributable to the momentary material interests of dominant social elites. They are endogenous to security policy, the traditional core of state sovereignty, in all of its dimensions. This is the paradox: inter-state competition may incentivize attacking global telecommunications networks, but actually taking those networks down would be immediately self-destructive and self-defeating.

Territorial states, no matter their size, depend to a greater or lesser degree on global networks to defend themselves and to project their power extraterritorially. The more states become entangled in global networks, the less likely they are to disable, degrade or destroy them (Nye 2017). This network effect may help explain why, in spite of repeated warnings of attacks on critical infrastructure, we have not yet witnessed systemic warfare by states that clearly have the capability of engaging in it. Borders in cyberspace are deepening and expanding, but they are only one part of a complex process of mutual entanglement.

Figure 3.1.
Suspected Government Users of Hacking Team Spyware

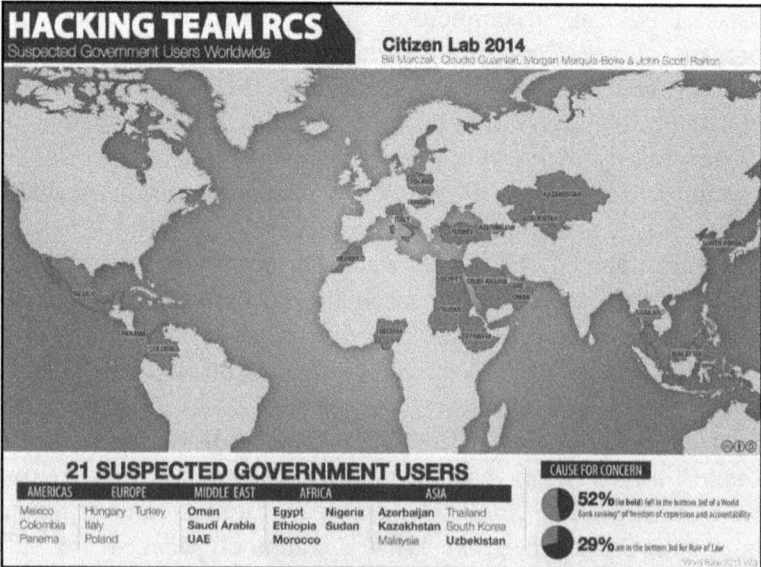

HACKING TEAM RCS
Suspected Government Users Worldwide

Citizen Lab 2014
Bill Marczak, Claudio Guarnieri, Morgan Marquis-Boire & John Scott Railton

21 SUSPECTED GOVERNMENT USERS

AMERICAS	EUROPE	MIDDLE EAST	AFRICA		ASIA	
Mexico	Hungary Turkey	Oman	Egypt	Nigeria	Azerbaijan	Thailand
Colombia	Italy	Saudi Arabia	Ethiopia	Sudan	Kazakhstan	South Korea
Panama	Poland	UAE	Morocco		Malaysia	Uzbekistan

CAUSE FOR CONCERN

52% (in bold) fall in the bottom 3rd of a World Bank ranking of freedom of expression and accountability

29% are in the bottom 3rd for Rule of Law

Note: This map shows 21 suspected government users of Hacking Team spyware, which employs RCS. They include some of the world's most notorious authoritarian regimes. This and the following figures are based on Citizen Lab research involving reverse engineering of malware samples received from targets and victims, followed by months of network scanning and measurement using techniques drawn from computer science and engineering to produce a "fingerprint" of country clients and the infrastructure used to support the operation of the commercial spyware.

Figure 3.2.
Suspected Government Users of Finfisher Spyware

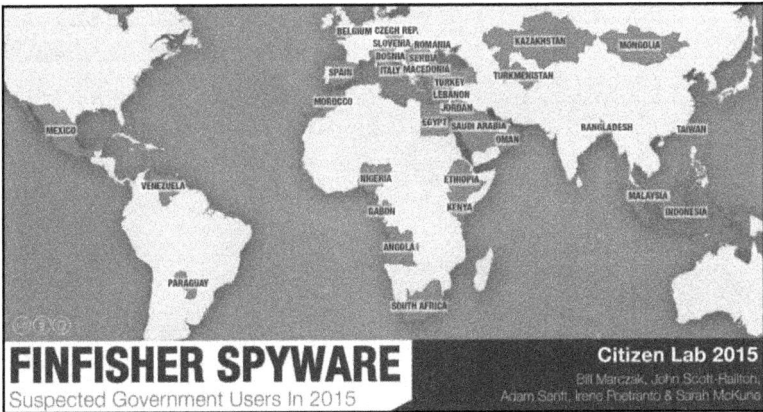

Note: This map shows the clients of Finfisher. As with Hacking Team clients, Finfisher sells its spyware to some of the world's most "closed" authoritarian regimes.

Figure 3.3. Foreign Espionage Campaigns Using Hacking Team Spyware and US Hosting Providers

Note: This map illustrates the foreign espionage infrastructure operating in the United States using Hacking Team software.

Figure 3.4. Mexican and Moroccan Circuits Used to Mask Attribution of Attacks

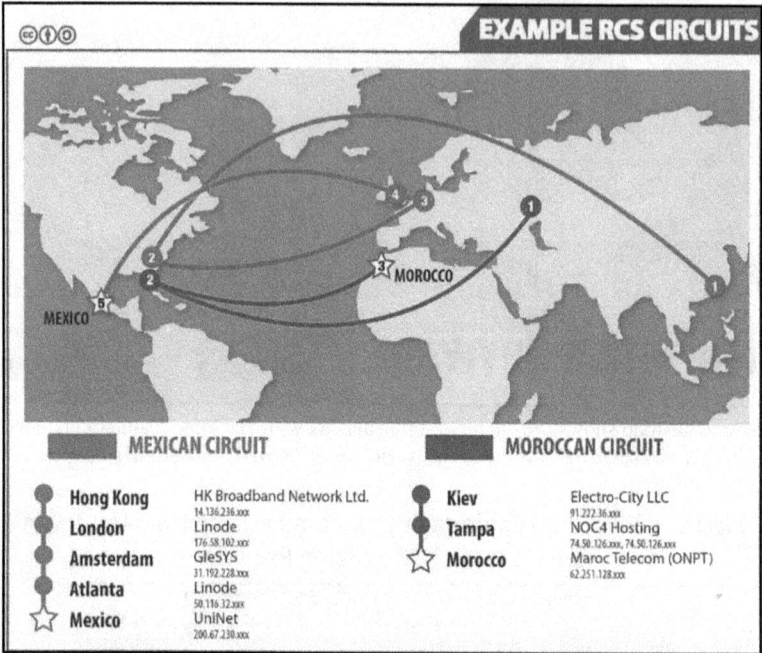

Note: This map illustrates how US-based cloud and networking service providers were used to attempt to mask attribution of two country-clients' use of Hacking Team software.

References

ASL19 and Psiphon. 2013. "Information Controls: Iran's Presidential Elections." *ASL19*. https://asl19.org/cctr/iran-2013election-report/.

Blue, V. 2012. "Hack In The Box: researcher reveals ease of Huawei router access." *ZDNet*, October 11. http://www.zdnet.com/article/hack-in-the-box-researcher-reveals-ease-of-huawei-router-access/.

Citizen Lab. 2014. "Communities @Risk: Targeted Digital Threats Against Civil Society." *Citizen Lab*, Report 48. https://targetedthreats.net/index.html.

Citizen Lab and ASL19. 2013. "After the Green Movement: Internet Controls in Iran, 2009-2012." *OpenNet Initiative Special Report*, March 11. https://opennet.net/sites/opennet.net/files/iranreport.pdf.

Cordesman, A., Sullivan, G., and Sullivan, W. 2007. "Lessons of the 2006 Israeli-Lebanon War." *Center for Strategic and International Studies*, Significant Issues Series, 29(4). https://csis.org/files/publication/120720_Cordesman_LessonsIsraeliHezbollah.pdf.

Dalek J., Kleemola K., Senft A., Parsons C., Hilts A., McKune S., Ng J.Q., Crete-Nishihata M., Scott-Railton J. and Deibert R. 2015. "A Chatty Squirrel: Privacy and Security Issues with UC Browser." *Citizen Lab*, Research Brief 55, May 21. https://citizenlab.org/2015/05/a-chatty-squirrel-privacy-and-security-issues-with-uc-browser/.

Deibert, R. 2012. "Social Media, Inc.: The Global Politics of Big Data." *World Politics Review*, June 19. http://www.worldpoliticsreview.com/articles/12065/social-media-inc-the-global-politics-of-big-data.

Deibert, R. 2015 "Authoritarianism Goes Global: Cyberspace under Siege." *Journal of Democracy* 26(3): 64-78.

Deibert, R., and Crete-Nishihata, M. 2012. "Global Governance and the Spread of Cyberspace Controls." *Global Governance* 18(3): 339-61.

Deibert, R., Palfrey J., Rohozinski, R., and Zittrain, J., eds. 2008. *Access Denied: The Practice and Policy of Internet Filtering.* Cambridge, MA: MIT Press.

Deibert, R., Palfrey J., Rohozinski, R., and Zittrain, J., eds. 2010. *Access Controlled: Policies and Practices of Internet Filtering and Surveillance.* Cambridge, MA: MIT Press.

Deibert, R., Palfrey J., Rohozinski, R., and Zittrain, J., eds. 2012. *Access Contested: Security, Resistance, and Identity in Asian Cyberspace.* Cambridge, MA: MIT Press.

Deibert, R., and Rohozinski, R. 2008. "Good for Liberty, Bad for Security? Internet Securitization and Global Civil Society." Pp. 123-65 in *Access Denied: The Practice and Policy of Internet Filtering*, edited by R. Deibert, J. Palfrey, R. Rohozinski, and J. Zittrain. Cambridge, MA: MIT Press.

Deibert, R. and Rohozinski, R. 2010. "Risking Security: The Policies and Paradoxes of Cyberspace Security." *International Political Sociology* 4(1):15-32.

Deibert, R., Rohozinski R., and Crete-Nishihata, M. 2012. "Cyclones in Cyberspace: Information Shaping and Denial in the 2008 Russia-Georgia War." *Security Dialogue* 43(1): 3-24.

Demchak, C., and Dombrowski, P. 2011. "Rise of a cybered Westphalian age." *Strategic Studies Quarterly* 5(1): 32-61.

Dombrowski, P. 2016. "China Wants to Draw Borders in Cyberspace." *New Perspectives Quarterly* 33(2): 38-42.

Drake, W., Cerf, V., and Kleinwachter, W. 2016. "Internet Fragmentation: An Overview." *World Economic Forum*, Future of the Internet Initiative Whitepaper.

http://www3.weforum.org/docs/WEF_FII_Internet_Fragmentation_An_Overview_2016.pdf.

FireEye. 2015. "HAMMERTOSS: Stealthy Tactics Define a Russian Cyber Threat Group." *FireEye Special Report.* https://www2.fireeye.com/rs/848-DID-242/images/rpt-apt29-hammertoss.pdf.

Friends Committee on National Legislation. 2015. "FNCL: Understanding Drones." *Friends Committee on National Legislation.* http://fcnl.org/issues/foreign_policy/understanding_drones/.

Harris, S. 2014. *@War: The Rise of the Military–Internet Complex.* Boston, MA: Eamon Dolan/Houghton Mifflin Harcourt.

Howard, P., Agarwal, S., and Hussain, M. 2011. "The Dictators" Digital Dilemma: When Do States Disconnect Their Digital Networks?" *Issues in Technology Innovation* 13:1–11. https://www.brookings.edu/research/the-dictators-digital-dilemma-when-do-states-disconnect-their-digital-networks/.

Johnson, D., and Post, D. 1996. "Law and Borders—The Rise of Law in Cyberspace." *Stanford Law Review* 48(5):1367-1402.

Knockel J., McKune S., and Senft, A. 2016. "Baidu's and Don'ts: Privacy and Security Issues in Baidu Browser." *Citizen Lab*, Research Brief 72, 23 February. https://citizenlab.org/2016/02/privacy-security-issues-baidu-browser/.

Knockel J., Senft A., and Deibert R. 2016. "Wup! There It Is: Privacy and Security Issues in QQ Browser." *Citizen Lab*, Research Brief 75, March 28. https://citizenlab.org/2016/03/privacy-security-issues-qq-browser/.

Lennon, M. 2015. "Russian Hacker Tool Uses Legitimate Web Services to Hide Attacks: FireEye." *SecurityWeek*, July 29. http://www.securityweek.com/russian-hacker-tool-uses-legitimate-web-services-hide-attacks-fire eye.

Lindsay, J. 2015a. "The Impact of China on Cybersecurity: Fiction and Friction." *International Security* 39(3): 7–47.

Lindsay, J. 2015b. "Tipping the Scales: The Attribution Problem and the Feasibility of Deterrence against Cyberattack." *Journal of Cybersecurity* 1(1): 53-67.

Marczak, B., Guarnieri, C., Marquis-Boire, M., and Scott-Railton, J. 2014a. "Hacking Team and the Targeting of Ethiopian Journalists." *Citizen Lab*, Research Brief 32, February 12. https://citizenlab.org/2014/02/hacking-team-targeting-ethiopian-journalists/.

Marczak B., Guarnieri, C., Marquis-Boire, M., and Scott-Railton, J. 2014b. "Mapping Hacking Team"s Untraceable Spyware." *Citizen Lab*, Research Brief 33, February 17. https://citizenlab.org/2014/02/mapping-hacking-teams-untraceable-spyware/.

Marczak, B., Guarnieri, C., Marquis-Boire, M., Scott-Railton, J., and McKune S. (2014) "Hacking Team"s US Nexus." *Citizen Lab*, Research Brief 35, February 28. https://citizenlab.org/2014/02/hacking-teams-us-nexus/.

Marczak, B., Scott-Railton, J., and McKune, S. 2015. "Hacking Team Reloaded? US-Based Ethiopian Journalists Again Targeted With Spyware." *Citizen Lab*, Research Brief 50, March 9. https://citizenlab.org/2015/03/hacking-team-reloaded-us-based-ethiopian-journalists-targeted-sp yware/.

Marczak, B., Scott-Railton, J., Poetranto, I., Senft, A., and McKune, S. 2015. "Pay No Attention to the Server behind the Proxy: Mapping FinFisher's Continuing Proliferation." *Citizen Lab*, Research Brief 65, October 15. https://citizenlab.org/2015/10/mapping-finfishers-continuing-proliferation/.

Marquis-Boire, M. 2012a. "From Bahrain with Love: FinFisher's Spy Kit Exposed?"

Citizen Lab, Research Brief 9, July 25. https://citizenlab.org/2012/07/from-bahrain-with-love-finfishers-spy-kit-exposed/.

Marquis-Boire M. 2012b. "Backdoors are Forever: Hacking Team and the Targeting of Dissent?" *Citizen Lab*, Research Brief 12, October 10. https://citizenlab.org/2012/10/backdoors-are-forever-hacking-team-and-the-targeting-of-dissent/.

Marquis-Boire, M. 2014. "Schrodinger's Cat Video and the Death of Clear-Text." *Citizen Lab*, Research Brief 46, August 15. https://citizenlab.org/2014/08/cat-video-and-the-death-of-clear-text/.

Marquis-Boire, M., Marczak, B., Guarnieri, C., and Scott-Railton, J. 2013a. "You Only Click Twice: FinFisher's Global Proliferation." *Citizen Lab*, Research Brief 15, March 13. https://citizenlab.org/2013/03/you-only-click-twice-finfishers-global-proliferation-2/.

Marquis-Boire M., Marczak B., Guarnieri C. and Scott-Railton J. 2013b. "For Their Eyes Only: The Commercialization of Digital Spying." *Citizen Lab*, Research Brief 17, April 30. https://citizenlab.org/2013/04/for-their-eyes-only-2/.

Marquis-Boire, M., Scott-Railton, J., Guarnieri, C., and Kleemola, K. 2014. "Police Story: Hacking Team's Government Surveillance Malware." *Citizen Lab*, Research Brief 41, June 24. https://citizenlab.org/2014/06/backdoor-hacking-teams-tradecraft-android-implant/.

Marquis-Boire, M., Marczak, B., and Guarnieri, C. 2012. "The SmartPhone Who Loved Me: FinFisher Goes Mobile." *Citizen Lab*, Research Brief 11, August 29. https://citizenlab.org/2012/08/the-smartphone-who-loved-me-finfisher-goes-mobile/.

Mozur, P. 2015. "Baidu and CloudFlare Boost Users Over China's Great Firewall." *The New York Times*, September 13. http://www.nytimes.com/2015/09/14/business/partnership-boosts-users-over-chinas-great-firewa ll.html?_r=0.

Nye, J., Jr. 2017. "Deterrence and Dissuasion in Cyberspace." *International Security* 41(3): 44-71.

Regalado, D., Villeneuve, N., and Scott-Railton, J. 2015. "Behind the Syrian Conflict's Digital Front Lines." *FireEye Special Report*, February 2015. https://www.fireeye.com/content/dam/fireeye-www/global/en/current-threats/pdfs/rpt-behind-the- syria-conflict.pdf.

Soldatov, A., and Borogan, I. 2015. *The Red Web: The Struggle between Russia's Digital Dictators and the New Online Revolutionaries*. New York: Public Affairs.

Scott-Railton, J., and Kleemola, K. 2015. "London Calling: Two Factor Authentication Phishing from Iran." *Citizen Lab*, Research Brief 61, August 27. https://citizenlab.org/2015/08/iran_two_factor_phishing/.

Stecklow, S. 2012. "Special Report: Chinese Firm Helps Iran Spy on Citizens." *Reuters*, March 22. http://www.reuters.com/article/us-iran-telecoms-idUSBRE82L0B820120322.

Small Media. 2015. "Iranian Internet Infrastructure and Policy Report." *The Rouhani Review (2013-2015)*, Special Edition. *Small Media*. https://smallmedia.org.uk/sites/default/files/u8/IIIP_Feb15.pdf.

Stiennon, R. 2016. "The Entire IT Security Landscape." *25th RSA Conference*, San Francisco, CA, March 18. https://www.youtube.com/watch?v=YYNM2VRmncE.

Tanase, S. 2015. "Satellite Turla: APT Command and Control in the Sky." *Securelist*, September 9. https://securelist.com/blog/research/72081/satellite-turla-apt-command-and-control-in-the-sky/.

Union of Concerned Scientists. 2016. "UCS Satellite Database." February 25. http://www.ucsusa.org/nuclear-weapons/space-weapons/satellite-database#.VyykWxUrKgQ.

Villeneuve, N. 2008. "Breaching Trust: An Analysis of Surveillance and Security Practices on China's TOM-Skype Platform." *Information Warfare Monitor*, 1 October. https://www.scribd.com/doc/13712715/Breaching-Trust-An-analysis-of-surveillance-and-security-practices-on-China-s-TOM-Skype-platform.

Vine, D. 2015. *Base Nation: How US Military Bases Abroad Harm America and the World*. New York: Henry Holt.

Vodafone. 2014. "Vodafone Law Enforcement Disclosure Report 2013/2014." https://www.vodafone.com/content/sustainabilityreport/2014/index.html.

Ward, S. 2014. "NEWSCASTER - An Iranian Threat Inside Social Media." *iSIGHT Partners*, May 28. https://www.isightpartners.com/2014/05/newscaster-iranian-threat-inside-social-media/.

Wege, C. 2012. "Hizballah's Counterintelligence Apparatus." *International Journal of Intelligence and Counter-Intelligence* 25(4): 771-85.

Zetter, K. 2014. *Countdown to Zero Day: Stuxnet and the Launch of the World's First Digital Weapon*. New York: Crown Publishers.

NORTH AND SOUTH

CHAPTER FOUR
Contesting Borders in the Arctic[1]

Klaus Dodds

Preamble

If and when we think about borders, and specifically the US-Canadian border, they are likely to be considered fixed and uncontroversial. Any typical map of North America represents three main international boundary lines—the US-Mexican border, the US-Canadian border, and a northern extension of the latter between the American state of Alaska and the Canadian territory of Yukon. These borders matter because they are recognised by the three state parties as delimiting national territories, sovereign authority and jurisdiction. While those states have negotiated with one another special border arrangements (facilitating approved mobility of trade and citizens, for example), the US-Canadian continental border is settled. However, if we journey further north, and focus on the maritime boundaries between the US and Canada, things appear less straightforward.

In the Arctic, as a consequence of a variety of factors including sea ice melt, globalisation, indigenous rights, and commercial opportunities, there is growing interest in how this region is bordered and defined. This sense of dynamism was captured in an infographic issued by the Washington, D.C.-based Wilson Center in December 2014. Under the banner headline, "I didn't know that! Arctic borders still aren't settled," it stipulates that, "Even with the world's longest peaceful border and advanced mapping capabilities, *Canada and the United States disagree about where their Arctic border begins and ends*, specifically in the Beaufort Sea" (emphasis in original). The underlying conceit appears to be one in which the reader is expected to be surprised that liberal democratic states such as Canada and the US have any border issues to discuss (see Figure 4.1).

1. My sincere thanks to Professor Robert Brym of the University of Toronto for extending an invitation to participate in the Third S. D. Clark Symposium on the Future of Canadian Society in November 2017 and for his skillful editing of this chapter. Thanks also to Grace Ramirez at the Department of Sociology at the University of Toronto for her support. Finally, my thanks to Jenny Kynaston at the Department of Geography, Royal Holloway, University of London, for redrawing Figure 4.2 and Figure 4.3.

Figure 4.1.
Surprising? Borders are Not Fixed; Sea, Ice and Seabed Intersect; The Arctic Is Inhabited by Human Communities, Flora and Fauna

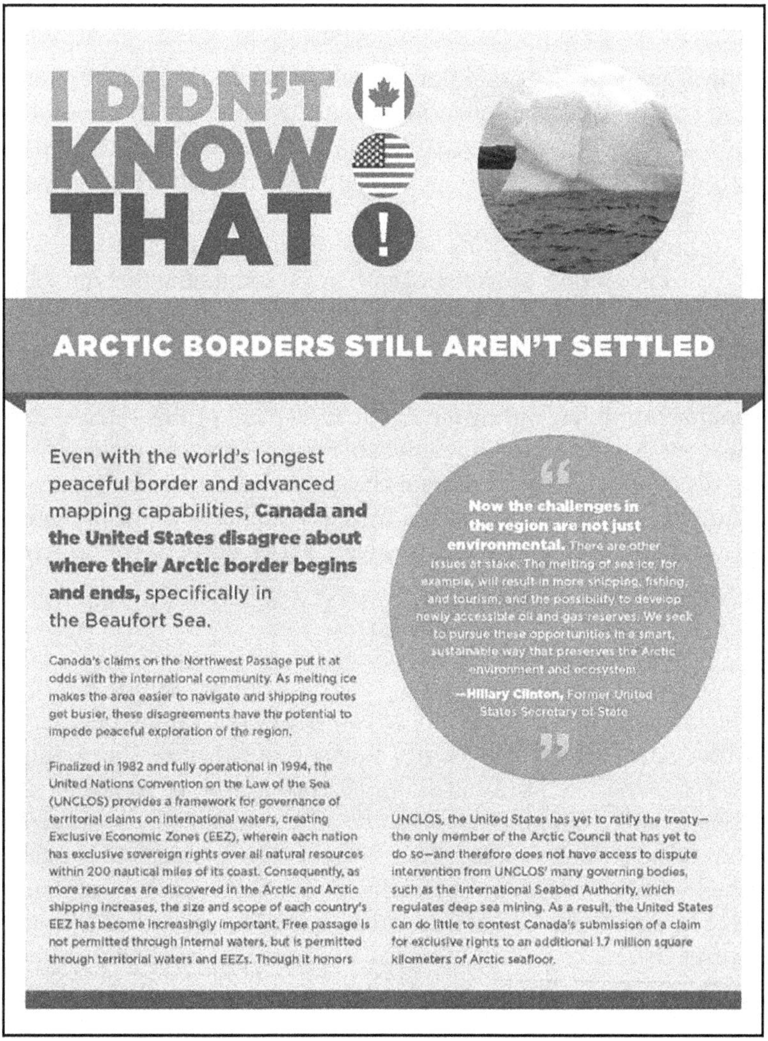

Source: Wilson Centre (2014).

The text therein alerts the reader that the United States and Canada disagree over the maritime delimitation of the Beaufort Sea, and dispute the international legal status of the Northwest Passage. The reader's attention is drawn to Canadian interests in establishing sovereign rights over an extended continental shelf, stretching ever closer towards the central Arctic Ocean (CAO). In 2018, Canada expects to submit materials to a UN body, the Commission on the Continental Shelf (CLCS), regarding a continental shelf claim. Until recently very few people had heard of the CLCS but this technical-scientific body is going to play an important role in helping to shape the sovereign rights of coastal states like Canada to vast areas of the seabed. The United States, as a non-party to the United Nations Convention on the Law of the Sea (UNCLOS), is not able to submit such a claim to the CLCS but this has not stopped it from mapping and surveying its seabed in the Arctic, Atlantic and Pacific Oceans.

The infographic provides an entrée into something that must appear desperately obscure to many readers. While the seabed in question is undeniably remote, it points to how active states like Canada are in maximizing their sovereign rights over territory, including possible resources. But in the Arctic Ocean, all of this interest and endeavor is occurring in the midst of concern that the region is being discombobulated by climate change and growing interest in its future by "outsiders," and this in turn has implications for the interests and rights of Indigenous peoples. Arctic borders are far from settled.

Introduction

The aforementioned infographic on Arctic borders is not an innocent intervention. It foregrounds two issues but avoids one. First, borders, and what might be reasonably thought of as "bordering," are processes, not fixed outcomes (Johnson et al. 2011; Jones and Johnson 2016). The border, let alone an internationally recognized boundary between two countries, is not static. Even the well-established and fully-functioning southern US-Canadian border is not just a line on a map but an assemblage of policies, practices and discourses that make possible a tightly integrated international boundary (Nicol 2015). Borderlines need to be maintained, surveyed and patrolled. For example, the International Boundary Commission for the US-Canadian border maintains a visible line through over 1,300 miles of forested land; the narrow vista is known colloquially as "the slash." It requires work crews cutting back vegetation along the border every four to five years depending on the vigour of regrowth.

The Alaskan-Canadian border has a separate border management regime in part because the growing season is shorter and the vegetation is shorter. There, the strip is approximately 20 feet wide.

Sometimes the US-Canadian border can be a site of controversy, as it was in 2017 when news broke of refugee seekers dying of hypothermia in the middle of a brutal winter. In particular areas of the shared border, such as in and around the St. Lawrence river, US-Canadian border management has created friction and conflict with cross-border Mohawk communities, which claim historic Indigenous sovereignty (Phaneuf 1979). Recent disputes over Indigenous sovereign rights have included protests over trans-shipment of radioactive material through Mohawk/Akwesasne territory and the intensification of maritime security measures, which have been implemented without the consultation of the Saint Regis Mohawk Tribal Council. The critically acclaimed film *Frozen River* (2008) addressed well the contested sovereign geographies of this riparian environment and the differential impact it had on particular white, Sioux and illegal immigrants.

These observations suggest that if and when the US and Canada agree on a maritime boundary in the northerly Beaufort Sea, it will require an ongoing process of consultation with Indigenous peoples as well as state-sponsored mapping, surveying, patrolling and administering. At the moment, there is no agreement as to where the line dividing the Beaufort Sea should begin, and without that agreement it is not possible to delimit territorial seas and exclusive economic zones in the disputed portion.

The roots of the international disagreement lie with an 1825 Treaty involving Russia (of which Alaska was then a part) and the UK. The treaty failed to establish a maritime boundary north of the coastline. The point about consultation lies in the context of the 1984 Inuvialuit Final Agreement (IFA) signed between Inuvialuit communities and Canada. It stipulates that local communities must be able to fully participate in decisions about conservation and economic development related to the Beaufort Sea. The United States believes that the boundary between the US and Canada in the Beaufort Sea should follow the equidistant principle. The Canadians maintain that the border should follow the 141st meridian and thus become a linear extension of the land border. At present, no agreement exists on how to proceed. Both countries believe that the Beaufort Sea contains valuable living and non-living resource potential.

All of which suggests that we are likely to see more Arctic border-work in the coming years. So while the infographic is right to

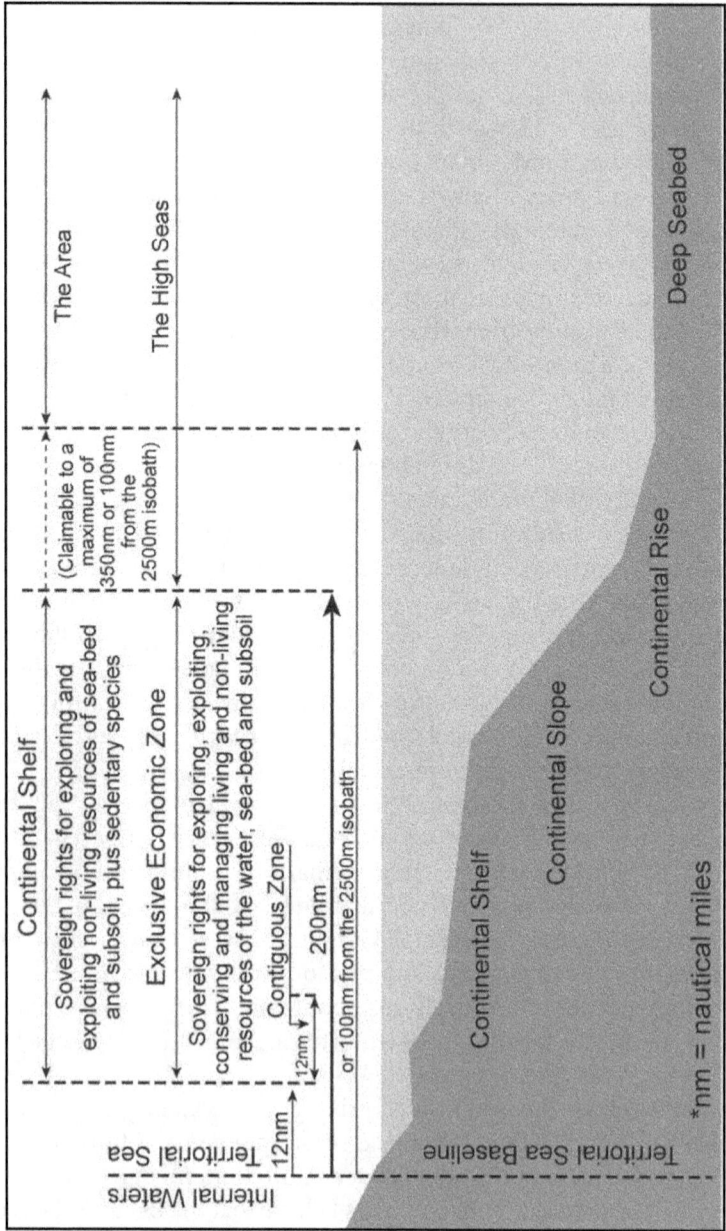

Figure 4.2. Zones of Maritime Rights

Continental Shelf
Sovereign rights for exploring and exploiting non-living resources of sea-bed and subsoil, plus sedentary species

Exclusive Economic Zone
Sovereign rights for exploring, exploiting, conserving and managing living and non-living resources of the water, sea-bed and subsoil

The Area

The High Seas

(Claimable to a maximum of 350nm or 100nm from the 2500m isobath)

Contiguous Zone

12nm

200nm

or 100nm from the 2500m isobath

Territorial Sea

12nm

Internal Waters

Continental Shelf

Continental Slope

Continental Rise

Deep Seabed

Territorial Sea Baseline

*nm = nautical miles

suggest that "Arctic borders still aren't settled," the nature of the "unsettlement" varies in geographical extent, geopolitical significance and legal sensitivity.

Borders can and do move, for example. Sometimes border shifts are proposed for perfectly peaceful reasons. In 2016, discussions about altering the mountainous border between northern Norway and Finland took place so as to "gift" a new high point to Finland on the eve of its 100th independence anniversary in 2017. After much public campaigning, the Norwegian government declined to do so, fearing that it might be unconstitutional as Article 1 of the Norwegian Constitution declares that the kingdom of Norway is "indivisible and inalienable." Although the mountain-swap proposal was no doubt well-intentioned, it reaffirms a basic geopolitical adage that nation-states rarely "give up" territory once it has been claimed and recognised by others.

Such rarity should not distract us from something less rooted and infinitely more mobile. Historically, a raft of border scholarship has made the point that sailors, pirates, buccaneers and their ships were "vectors of law" that allowed sponsoring states to extend their sovereign authority over seas and oceans (Benton 2009). Moving offshore, over the last twenty years we have witnessed a slow and steady legal-technical process of continental shelf delimitation as icebreakers and survey ships play a crucial role in tracking up and down the Arctic Ocean. As they measure and assess underwater geology and take stock of bathymetry, these voyages are integral to coastal state expansion of sovereign rights.

These efforts consolidate a massive expansion of state sovereignty in the maritime realm courtesy of UNCLOS, which entered into force in 1994. Coastal states have been able to appropriate exclusive economic zones and territorial seas, and establish an array of sovereign rights over seabed, islands and water column (Rothwell and Stephens 2016; see Figure 4.2). In the case of outer continental shelves in the Arctic Ocean, it is fully expected that the Canadian, Danish and Russian technical submissions to the CLCS will overlap one another. The three coastal states will engage in formal negotiations in the expectation that they will resolve where their respective sovereign rights begin and end. All three believe that, under Article 76 of UNCLOS, they will demonstrate that their sovereign rights will extend beyond 350 nautical miles from the coastal baseline (Dodds 2010). The areas involved are vast, and will encompass much of the Arctic Ocean seabed (Jensen 2015). For all the speculation about Russia and its strategic intentions (recall the infographic cited earlier was produced prior to Russia's annexation of Crimea in March 2014), most commentators expect future negotiations over Arctic outer continental shelves to be consensual.

The second point relevant to our discussion is that the three examples listed by the infographic involve the intersection of sea, ice and the seabed. The terrain of the maritime Arctic is integral to any discussion of borders. The intersection of law, territory and geopolitics helps to make and remake the Arctic (Steinberg et al. 2015). Territory is not simply a passive backdrop to those intersectional relationships. Canada and the United States disagree over whether the Northwest Passage (NWP) is part of Canada's "internal waters" (Lajeunesse 2016). The US position, which is shared by other parties including the EU, is that the waterways of the Canadian Arctic are international straits, where third parties enjoy far greater freedoms of transit and navigation than in internal waters. Part of the long-standing argument pertaining to the NWP is the role of ice-covered waters, and whether they have not only prevented regular transit shipping in the past but also acted as an exceptional hazard requiring the Canadian government as the relevant coastal state to act as an "exceptional" environmental steward (Burke 2017). So while both sides appeal to international law as a guide, the historic and contemporary presence of sea ice is pivotal to these rival legal, political and cultural narratives (Griffiths 1987).

What emerges from this discussion about the NWP is not just a multitude of legal and political argumentation, but something rooted in the geophysical. Continental shelves, ocean seabed, maritime passages, ice-covered waters and the polar water column provide raw material for legal and political intervention and strategy (Steinberg and Peters 2015). The physical geographies of the maritime Arctic and their capacity to block, enable and frustrate the spatial strategies of territorial states matter. If past experience suggests anything it is that the mobility of people and things has been a powerful platform for the expansion of law and opportunities for data capture about those mobile objects. The changing fate of Arctic sea ice is integral to many discussions concerning the future of the Arctic, not least in determining future regulatory patterns of mobility and resource exploitation. Arctic states, including Canada, Denmark/Greenland, Norway, Russia and the United States represent themselves as Arctic Ocean coastal states with substantial resource and strategic interests in their territorial seas, exclusive economic zones and continental shelves (Dodds 2013). They are predominant in ongoing discussions about the future management of the central Arctic Ocean, which will also involve extra-territorial parties such as China and the European Union in the long-term (Pin and Huntingdon 2016).

The third relevant element the infographic raises is something it does *not* address. Nowhere in the description that follows about Arctic borders is there any recognition that the Arctic is inhabited by human communities and flora and fauna. Borders and border delimitation are presented as legal-technical phenomena involving relevant coastal states and their geopolitical/strategic interests. Under the title of "Contested Canadian claims to the Arctic," the three examples (Beaufort Sea, Northwest Passage and Continental Shelf) show no recognition that Indigenous peoples in Canada have substantial land and maritime claims, and that they contest the sovereign authority of the Government of Canada to act exclusively in such matters (Nicol 2010, Powell 2010). Agreements with Indigenous peoples exist. They stipulate Canada's obligation to consult Indigenous people and respect Indigenous rights onshore and offshore (see section 35 of the 1982 Canadian Constitution).

The right to consult does not apply just to border issues like those involving the US and Canada in the Beaufort Sea. Underwater objects that were lost but now found in "Canadian waters" are also enrolled in this nation (Crown) to nation (Indigenous peoples) partnership. In 2018 the National Maritime Museum and the Canadian Museum of History collaborated on a "Death in the Ice" exhibition, which considers the material and imaginative legacies of the doomed Victorian-era Sir John Franklin expedition. In the last few years, the remains of Franklin's ships HMS *Erebus* and *Terror* were discovered in Canadian waters. Some of the artefacts are displayed in the exhibition, but even before its official opening it was mired in controversy. Who owns the artefacts? Parks Canada, which was instrumental in leading the recent search for the ships, argued that it was a matter for the federal government citing a 1997 bilateral agreement with the UK about the remains of the ship. However, the Inuit Heritage Trust contends that the government of Nunavut should have been consulted about ownership. In other words, the remains of the ships were not straightforwardly Canadian. In 2017, the UK government formally transferred ownership of the ships to Canada and the Trudeau government has entered into formal discussions with relevant Inuit organizations.

It follows that reasoned discussion of Arctic borders must recognize that it is a complex subject. Even if we decline to extend our remit to flora and fauna, a case could be made that what constitutes the Arctic is ever more contested, thanks in no small part to the warming of the region. Melting permafrost, sea ice shrinkage, ocean acid-ification and alteration to the local and regional albedo is producing amplification and perturbation. It is not too fanciful to claim that the Arctic is being "scrambled" in the sense that ecosystem change is disrupting food supplies, habitats, migratory routes of land and sea-based animals and settlement patterns. Scientists warn increasingly of invasive species, habitat domain disruption and the "greening" of the Arctic (Arctic Council 2017). Where the Arctic begins and ends is also being scrambled (Dodds and Nuttall 2016). Bio-geographi-cal borders are being re-drawn as tundra retreats and boreal forest advances. The shrinkage of Arctic sea ice is also promising to reveal further potential for maritime space to be reimagined and reorga-nized as open polar sea as opposed to frozen polar desert. Nowadays, it is commonplace to read of the potential for commercial fishing in the central Arctic Ocean. This would have been unthinkable in the 1970s.

For the purposes of this paper, attention will focus on three the-matic areas. Initially, some observations will be offered regarding recent scholarship on borders and geopolitics. Thereafter, attention turns to Arctic borders with specific focus on Arctic states and their bordering strategies. Finally, mindful of the year of writing, the pa-per concludes with some reflections on Indigenous geopolitics and Canada 150, and ruminates on how borders are corporeal as much as material, legal and representational. If we are interested in how Arctic borders are contested then we need to consider Arctic states such as Canada and their own border work in the broader context of structural racism (Milloy 1999), racial violence and assimilation (Thobani 2007), settler colonialism (Baker 2009), entrenched in-equality (Porter 1965) and Cold War geopolitics (Lackenbauer and Farish 2007).

Borders, Geopolitics and Critical Border Studies
Over the last 20 years, the fields of critical geopolitics and critical border studies have contributed to a rich and diverse body of work. What we can take from this literature are several fundamentals—the border is never just a static line; the border is crucial to expressions of identity politics and the identification and policing of the inside/outside of territorial states; the border is shaped by the intersection of material and infrastructural geographies; and the border is always embodied and corporal. In other words, experiences of the border are unevenly distributed. In a post-9/11 environment, nation-states including Canada and the United States have invested heavily in bor-

der management in the light of fear of more terrorism, crime and unregulated migration (Panquin and James 2014). While ambulatory networks provoke concern, the border makes itself manifest in a diverse array of sites and spaces, operating far beyond the formal border with other nation-states.

The border makes itself manifest in particular environments and locales. It always involves placing and displacing. Borders are, therefore, never simply lines on the map nor are they simply made manifest through security infrastructure and practices such as fences, barbed wire, surveillance towers and watching and border patrolling respectively. Borders are more productively thought of as always institutionally thick, spatially multi-faceted and embodied. The border is at once topographical and topological—finding expression in particular areas of the earth like international boundary lines between sovereign states but also corporeal and relational in the sense of making their presence felt on some bodies more than others. Relationships with the border extend far beyond the formal border line, as people of colour and migrants often note that it is they who fall under the watchful gaze of citizen and officials alike (De Leon 2015; Neyers 2012).

Borders can and do regularise the relationship between the state, the citizen and the alien but they also generate an array of alternative border economies and solidarities. The border might help define the limits of state hospitality but it also generates opportunities for others to circumvent, contest and capitalise on. In the fall of 2015, for example, Norwegian citizens offered support to Afghan, Kurdish, Syrian and Iraqi refugees crossing the Norwegian-Russian border. Over 5,000 people sought asylum in Norway that year, and in 2016 local Norwegian citizens and support groups protested a Norwegian government decision to forcibly return some of those who had crossed the border with valid Russian visas. Forced returns soon became politically impossible, and again local citizens and churches offered hospitality and support to those affected.

By 2017, the Russian authorities put an end to asylum seekers cycling to Norway and refugees transferred to reception centres across Norway. In the meantime, the Norwegian government invested in new security fencing, which proved divisive with local residents who argued that it might unsettle existing cross-border relationships with Russia. The Norwegian-Russian borderlands have had their own distinct agreement dating from 2010, which created a visa-free border zone allowing residents either side of the border to enter in and out of that zone. It coincided with an agreement between the two countries over the maritime delimitation of the Barents Sea. So from a local resident's point of view, unsettling a national border agreement had immediate implications for everyday life.

Bordering and Boundary-Making in the Arctic

A series of photographs of the planting of a Russian flag at the bottom of the central Arctic Ocean in August 2007 precipitated a wave of commentary warning of a new scramble for the Arctic. While we can speculate about whether the febrile media and political reaction would have been similar if the flag in question had been that of the United Nations, the event itself coincided with news of a record low in Arctic sea ice distribution. Diminishing sea ice in combination with stories of new trade routes and a treasure-house of oil and gas fed a geographical imagination positing the Arctic as an ungoverned resource frontier awaiting exploration and exploitation. For all the geopolitical hype, many commentaries neglected to mention that the maritime Arctic was subject to the legal framework of UNCLOS. Far from being divorced from governance structures, the Arctic Ocean coastal states enjoyed sovereign rights over considerable areas of the maritime Arctic, and were actively positioning themselves as environmental stewards as well as sovereign actors (Dodds 2010).

However, the scrambling discourses did arguably provoke Arctic Ocean coastal states such as Canada and Russia to articulate, frame and implement spatial strategies designed to remind domestic and international audiences that they were Arctic Ocean coastal states. Domestically, Canadian Prime Minister Stephen Harper emerged as the most prominent advocate of Canadian Arctic sovereignty, with annual summer trips to the Canadian North designed to highlight the scale and extent of that sovereign authority (Dodds and Nuttall 2016). New plans and strategies were drawn up and publicised, including spending commitments on military and civilian infrastructure in the Arctic. Internationally, the Arctic Ocean coastal states met in Greenland to develop a common position regarding their role as environmental stewards in the maritime Arctic and to reaffirm the importance of UNCLOS and the "Law of the Sea" (in recognition of the United States' non-ratification of UNCLOS) in providing an orderly legal framework. Four out of the five Arctic Ocean coastal states also committed themselves to following UNCLOS rules for the definition and delimitation of the outer limits of their continental shelves (Article 76). In what was called the Ilulissat Declaration, Canada, Denmark/Greenland, Norway, Russia and the United States committed themselves to the following:

> Notably, the law of the sea provides for important rights and obligations concerning the delineation of the outer limits of the continental shelf, the protection of the marine environment, including ice-covered areas, freedom of navigation, marine scientific research, and other uses of the sea. We remain committed to this legal framework and to the orderly settlement of any possible overlapping claims. This framework provides a solid foundation for responsible management by the five coastal States and other users of this Ocean through national implementation and application of relevant provisions. We therefore see no need to develop a new comprehensive international legal regime to govern the Arctic Ocean. We will keep abreast of the developments in the Arctic Ocean and continue to implement appropriate measures (Ilulissat Declaration 2008).

The Declaration was intended to counter any suggestion that the maritime Arctic was either thinly governed and/or riven with dangerous historic border disputes over sea and islands. The formal "disputes" affecting the maritime Arctic in May 2008 (the date of the declaration) included the unresolved status of the Northwest Passage, the unsettled marine delimitation of the Beaufort Sea and Barents Sea, and the disputed ownerships of Hans Island involving Canada and Denmark. The definition and delimitation of outer continental shelves in the Arctic was ongoing and the international waters of the central Arctic Ocean had not attracted sustained international attention.

However orderly the UNCLOS framework may appear at first glance, there are likely to be contested borders in the delimitation of outer continental shelves. Under Article 76 of UNCLOS, coastal states such as Canada, Denmark and Russia can collect geophysical and oceanographic materials in accordance with stipulated procedures. Rules exist for how coastal states can extend their sovereign rights over the continental shelf, involving distance, depth and seabed geology. Put concisely, Article 76 outlines a process by which coastal states can submit materials to the UN Commission on the Continental Shelf (CLCS) for the purpose of obtaining a recommendation regarding delimitation. The CLCS does not issue legal judgements but if the coastal state follows the recommendation from the Commission, then the outer limits of the continental shelf become final and binding.

Where things become more complicated is when the delimitation of outer continental shelves involves overlapping submissions. In the case of the Arctic Ocean, it is well understood that submissions from Canada, Denmark/Greenland and Russia are likely to overlap. The CLCS has considered submissions from Russia (2001 and 2013) and Denmark/Greenland (2013) but not from Canada. The CLCS does not involve itself in legal disputes, so in the case of extended continental shelves in the Arctic Ocean, the three parties will have to negotiate with one another. All three parties have invested much time and money mapping the Arctic Ocean seabed. They believe, for example, that their sovereign rights extend all the way to the seabed around the North Pole. Ultimately, if the process outlined in Article 76 is followed then the three will eventually agree to a trilateral accommodation of their respective outer continental shelf submissions.

The negotiation has not formally begun because the CLCS has yet to receive the Canadian submission pertaining to the Arctic Ocean. When it begins, it will involve more than the three main state parties. The delimitation of the outer or extended continental shelf matters to other state parties because under Article 77 of UNCLOS all relevant coastal states enjoy exclusive rights over the continental shelf. Articles 76 and 77 represent in short the furthest extension of sovereign rights of the coastal states. Thereafter, the remaining seabed forms part of "The Area" and falls under the jurisdiction of the International Seabed Authority as far as resource exploration and exploitation are concerned. The Area is in effect a common heritage of humankind and in the case of the central Arctic Ocean there might be a few small regions that will be classified as part of The Area.

As noted earlier, the United States is not a state party to UNCLOS so thus far it has not been able to make a formal submission to the Commission. However, it has proceeded under the assumption that relevant articles on the continental shelf codify customary international law. The US is thus delineating its continental shelf, including areas that go beyond the Exclusive Economic Zone and extended continental shelf. In other words, the US can delineate on the basis of customary international law but cannot secure the stamp of "final and binding." As Article 76(8) notes, "the Commission shall make recommendations to coastal States on matters related to the establishment of the outer limits of their continental shelf. The limits of the shelf established by a coastal state on the basis of these recommendations shall be final and binding."

What UNCLOS privileges, by its very nature, is coastal states and their sovereign rights on the one hand and on the other hand the interests of third (state) parties moving through the territorial waters and exclusive economic zones of coastal states. It creates rights for and obligations on state parties, and a distinct zonation of the seas and oceans. The further from the coastline, the more the sovereign rights of the appurtenant coastal state are checked and balanced with regard to other parties. Comparatively speaking, the Arctic and Southern Oceans were not given a great deal of prominence during the long negotiations that led to UNCLOS (1973–1982). UNCLOS was envisaged as a global legal framework for all the world's oceans and seas.

As international attention has grown, it is possible that the governance of the Arctic Ocean could become more controversial. One example will suffice. Article 234 of UNCLOS acknowledges that ice-covered areas might raise additional challenges to shipping and pollution control. Accordingly, the article stipulates that coastal states such as Canada and Russia can

> adopt and enforce nondiscriminatory laws and regulations for the prevention, reduction, and control of marine pollution from vessels in ice-covered areas within the limits of the exclusive economic zone, where particularly severe climatic conditions and the presence of ice covering such areas for most of the year create obstructions or exceptional hazards to navigation, and pollution of the marine environment could cause major harm to or irreversible disturbance of the ecological balance (UNCLOS 1982).

Coastal states are allowed to impose additional regulations on international shipping but they do so because of the presence of ice-covered areas for "most of the year." If sea ice continues to diminish, would other parties ignore and/or resist such measures? Could Article 234 in the future become mired in disputes involving the spatial extent of coastal state authority to impose environmental/pollution control measures on transit parties?

While we can speculate about what might happen to the Arctic Ocean in the future, it is notable that shortly after the May 2008 Ilulissat Declaration of the five Arctic Ocean coastal states, a Circumpolar Inuit Declaration on Sovereignty in the Arctic was released (Circumpolar Inuit Declaration 2009). Challenging the exclusive authority of Arctic Ocean coastal states, the Declaration challenged those states to respect Inuit values, interests, wishes and to ensure Indigenous participation. Arguably, the Declaration spelled out the legal position of Indigenous peoples in the maritime Arctic by advocating a transnational identity that spans the North American and Euro-Asian Arctic. Legal authorities such as Michael Byers argue that the Inuit Declaration, when taken alongside the UN Declaration on the Rights of Indigenous Peoples, represents a real challenge to the limits of the relevant coastal states (Byers 2013). As Article 4.2 of the Inuit Declaration notes:

> The conduct of international relations in the Arctic and the resolution of international disputes in the Arctic are not the sole preserve of Arctic states or other states; they are also within the purview of the Arctic's indigenous peoples. The development of international institutions in the Arctic, such as multi-level governance systems and indigenous peoples' organizations, must transcend Arctic states' agendas on sovereignty and sovereign rights and the traditional monopoly claimed by states in the area of foreign affairs (Circumpolar Inuit Declaration 2009).

The net result of this declaration is to caution those who assume that the future management of the maritime Arctic will involve only Arctic Ocean state parties. While formal boundary disputes involve Canada and Denmark (Hans Island) and Canada and the United States (Beaufort Sea), the Inuit Declaration is intended to remind Canadian, Danish and US audiences that Inuit are active transnational Arctic actors with interests in shipping, fishing and environmental protection. Other matters of jurisdiction involving transit rights regarding the NSR and NWP, and the uncertain legal status of the maritime areas around the Norwegian archipelago of Svalbard will require further negotiation and compromise.

Non-Arctic states such as China and South Korea enjoy certain navigation rights and are entitled to be involved in negotiations involving areas beyond national jurisdiction given their interests in high seas fisheries in the Central Arctic Ocean and mineral resources in any seabed classified as part of The Area. In July 2015, the Arctic Ocean coastal states signed a declaration agreeing to prevent their flagged vessels from conducting commercial fishing in the central Arctic Ocean until regulations were in place to manage such activity. Thereafter, the five state parties engaged with extra-territorial actors including China, the European Union, Iceland, Japan and South Korea. A high seas fisheries agreement was concluded in 2017. In effect, it places a moratorium on fishing activity in the CAO for at least sixteen years. The expectation is that, in the meantime, a regional fisheries management organization will be put in place to regulate development of commercial fishing.

Ultimately, what has transpired is an accommodation between coastal states and extra-territorial state parties with some recognition that Indigenous peoples of the Arctic need to be consulted. In 2015, the UN agreed to develop a new global instrument for the protection of marine biodiversity in areas beyond national jurisdiction. While designed to address gaps in governance and regulation, the central Arctic Ocean will require a strong consensus of opinion regarding marine conservation to prevail in the face of uncertainty regarding fish stock migration and maritime accessibility. Arctic maritime borders could still prove contentious if existing forms of circumpolar co-operation (as embodied by forums such as the Arctic Council) and international treaties (the Spitzbergen Treaty and UNCLOS) are unable to manage a diverse group of regional and extra-regional stakeholders.

Bordering and De-Bordering Indigenous Bodies

Thus far, much of the discussion has been dominated by the interests and visions of sovereign territorial states. While Arctic borders have practical and formal variability, the contemporary operational space of the Arctic is more complex than envisaged during the Cold War period when the region was exploited, militarised, policed and securitised by Arctic states and their sanctioned actors. The position of Indigenous peoples was often uncomfortable. In the North American Arctic, northern communities were on the one hand mobilised as a "living embodiment" of sovereign presence (in some cases enrolled in military units such as the Canadian Rangers) and yet on the other hand subject to forced relocation, structural racism, and assimilationist policies. Such policies, we could argue, were unquestionably bordering in the sense of Indigenous peoples being ordered, classified and dis-placed throughout Alaska and the Canadian North.

Thus, when the 2009 Circumpolar Inuit Declaration on Sovereignty in the Arctic spoke of the need to ensure that Inuit and other northern peoples were consulted and treated as partners, it occurred against a backdrop of resistance to centuries of Euro-American settler colonialism and boundary-making projects, involving land theft, dispossession, and infrastructural investment designed to advance the borders of Anglo-Canadian settlement. For much of Canada's political history, culminating in the celebration of the 150th anniversary of Confederation, the North has been appropriated, bordered, exploited and settled. The entry of the Yukon and Northwest Territories into Confederation in 1898 and 1870 respectively represented a shift in sovereign authority away from the Hudson's Bay Company toward the Canadian state. It was not until April 1999 that the Northwest Territories were decisively altered with the creation of a new territory, Nunavut, which followed on from the 1993 Nunavut Land Claims Agreement. The latter gave title to Inuit-owned lands encompassing 350,000 square kilometres and represents the largest aboriginal land settlement claim in Canadian history. The Nunavut Act also established self-governance in Nunavut and recognized the Inuit as traditional and current users of resources and wildlife as well as allowing them to engage with other stakeholders for non-renewable resource development.

On its face, the establishment of Nunavut represented a different sort of Arctic border (see Figure 4.3). The creation of Nunavut was the culmination of more than 20 years of negotiation with Indigenous peoples. It reaffirmed the North as a site of border-work—territory as something to be controlled, distributed and divided—and, critically, where obligations and rights were specified within the newly

Figure 4.3. New Types of Arctic Border

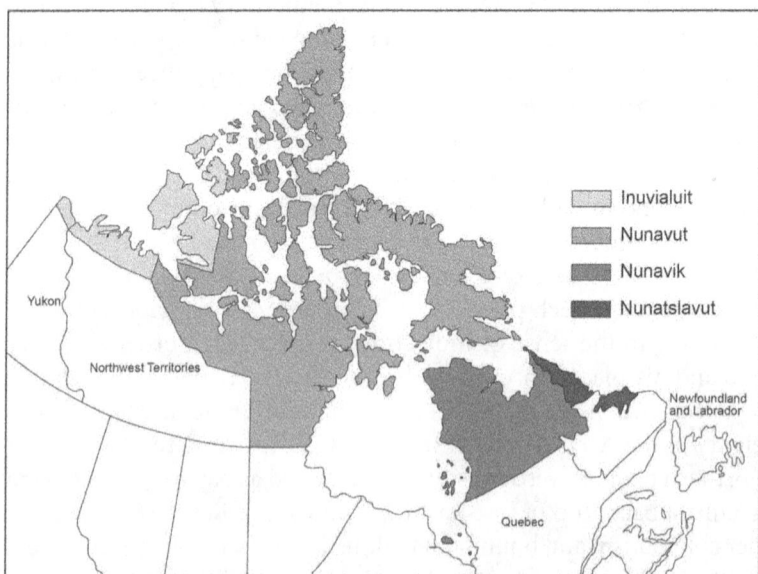

created territory. Since its establishment, however, controversy has existed with Nunavut Tunngavik Incorporated (NTI), the organization that represents the Inuit under the Nunavut Land Claim Agreement. Allegedly, the federal agreement has been failing to fulfill its obligations. In May 2015, NTI and the Harper government reached an out-of-court settlement concerning the lawsuit brought by NTI. It implicitly recognized that the implementation of the 1993 Nunavut Land Claims Agreement required substantial and sustained financial support, in the process highlighting the uneasy relationship between federal and territorial-level governance and border management.

In other words, for all the Canadian sovereignty talk by the Stephen Harper government, it was failing to invest in northern governance and civilian infrastructure as opposed to "sovereignty exercises," military hardware, underwater surveillance in the NWP and border security (Abele 2016).

But perhaps there was something else here that made itself more manifest in the recent Canada 150 celebrations: the ambivalent position of the Canadian North and its residents within the geographical imagination of southern Canadians including Prime Ministers. Hashtags such as #Reoccupation and #Resistance150 have generated considerable social media and traditional media coverage, explicitly challenging the "bordering" of Canadian history and geography.

For all the claims to significance of the North within Canadian national identity and sovereignty projects, it is a vast region that few Canadians will actually visit let alone inhabit (*Globe and Mail* 2014). If there is an imaginary border at play then perhaps it pivots around the register of apprehension (is Canadian sovereign territory in the north vulnerable to perfidious others?) and incomprehension (is it simply cold, underpopulated and expensive?). As Nunavut-based performance artist, Laakkuluk Williamson Bathory mused:

> The North is an extremely cold place, barren actually, without out a single tree in sight. You walk on the streets that are not even paved and you go into the stores and you pay exorbitant fees for things like milk and eggs and lettuce. Prices that are four or five times higher than any city in the South. And the people that you see in the aisles of the store are people who have the highest statistics of all the worst things. Highest suicide rates, the highest rates of unemployment, the lowest rates of education. It's an extremely difficult life here in the North. . . . For somebody like me who is racialized in mainstream Canadian society, I always have to describe who

I am, where I come from, and why (quoted in CBC 2014).

As a Greenlandic artist living and working in Iqaluit, Bathory makes a case for the border as something inherently embodied. It is affecting and intensely felt—something that separates and stratifies her and other indigenous peoples away from mainstream (predominantly white, Anglophone, settler-colonial) Canadian society. The Arctic border transmogrifies from being something rooted in place to an altogether more mobile assemblage of ideas, policies and practices that can and does make itself manifest far away from the Arctic/Canadian North. As Bathory notes, there are limits to assimilationist logics as Indigenous peoples are asked to account for their background, names and heritage. So when former Prime Minister Stephen Harper declared "We are a northern nation," he didn't stop to articulate who the "we" involved, and how and where Canadians might be enrolled in this national identity project.

As Indigenous activists noted throughout the planning and implementation of the Canada 150 celebrations, Indigenous peoples were living in the North for thousands of years before Confederation. When Canadian prime ministers speak of northern identities and northern nationalism, they don't dwell on the legacies of residential schools, racism, gendered violence, assimilation and a lack of basic infrastructure. If bordering strategies are at play, then they involve an Arctic which emptied out of a complex history and geography of militarism, pollution, under-investment and displacement, often in the name of addressing "the Indian problem." It is an Arctic where many southern Canadians can grow up with little awareness of what specific legislation such as the 1876 Indian Act entailed for Indigenous peoples in terms of their education, welfare and citizenship rights. Notwithstanding the work of the Truth and Reconciliation Commission on the legacy of residential schools and segregation, no northern communities were left untouched by this social-cultural border-work of the Canadian territorial state (Truth and Reconciliation Commission of Canada 2015).

As part of speaking against the epistemic violence of Canada 150, Indigenous activists mobilised different stories about Canada. They gave all Canadians the opportunity to learn about the vicarious nature of borders and bordering. Extending far beyond the Arctic region as defined by a line of latitude or territorial boundary line, this bordering asks us to question what is at stake—a vision of reconciliation where the everyday experiences of Indigenous peoples in the Arctic and further south are subsumed within logics of assimilation and reconciliation, logics in which Indigenous peoples would become "Canadianized" (sic) and embrace Canadian values and practices. For Indigenous scholars, #Colonialism150 and #Resistance150 are opportunities to highlight enduring colonial settler dynamics, which position northern peoples as equal treaty partners welcoming Canadian benevolence.

What might de-bordering the Canadian North/Arctic look and feel like? For one thing, it might start by recognising that for too long stories about Arctic borders have privileged territorial states and their strategies and interests. It might involve different stories about periodization, with due recognition of multiple temporalities involving millennia and not simply the last 150 years, let alone the last decade (McGhee 2008). Second, it would involve an acknowledgement that Indigenous peoples in the North were neither victims nor willing partners of the Crown and federal government. What the last 400 years of Indigenous-British-French-Canadian relations reveal is something inherently more complicated involving resistance, accommodation and negotiation on the basis of Canada being invited to enter into a relationship with First Nations, tribal and Indigenous peoples. Third, the renaming of places to reflect their Indigenous origins and recognition that some places rendered invisible by colonial settlers need to be restored to their former significance as recognized and named by Indigenous peoples. In other words, place names not only signify location but also help to shift the bordering of human and physical geographies. In 2017, Google confirmed that Google Maps and Earth had been updated with an additional 3000 Canadian Indigenous place-names added to maps of Canada (CBC 2017). Finally, it will involve more humility, listening (rather than talking) and appreciation that the story of Arctic borders and border-work is not always one "we" get to tell.

Epilogue

My rumination lacks a neat conclusion. "Our" stories have limits; we emphasise some places, relationships and places more than others. The Arctic border is anything but fixed, and it reveals uneven topographies both physical and corporeal. The physical terrain of the region clearly matters when it comes to shaping the prevailing legal framework governing the zonation of the maritime Arctic (Steinberg and Kristoffersen 2017). Coastal states such as Canada and Russia loom large in this rendition of borders, and their border-work is noteworthy when it comes to protecting their exclusive economic zones and extending sovereign rights over the continental shelf. International legal measures have encroached further on the seabed and water column of the Arctic Ocean. As a political technology, the legal migrates, settles and colonizes space. The intersection of sea ice, prevailing darkness, and the cold are elemental in this border-work, contributing to facilitation and occasional frustration of the expansion of the sovereign rights of territorial states.

The Beaufort Sea and the undetermined maritime border between the US and Canada involve an area of disagreement of about 625 square miles. On face value, it appears to be an area of disagreement requiring bilateral negotiation. No one expects the two countries to become embroiled in conflict over this matter but it could be highly controversial in both countries. Indigenous peoples in the Arctic have rights over water and ice. The delimitation of a maritime boundary between the two countries has implications for local communities on both sides of any border. Under Section 35 of the Canadian Constitution, every government has an obligation to respect and protect Indigenous peoples and their rights; land claim agreements across Canada facilitate the sharing of territories but do not extinguish Indigenous rights over land, sea and seabed. Can Canada cede any maritime territory to the US if it violates the interests and rights of Indigenous peoples? All of this occurs against a backdrop of increasing international interest in these waters from fishing and resource extraction to commercial access to the Northwest Passage.

But as the penultimate section of this essay suggests, borders and bordering are also felt. They do more than enclose and exclude material spaces and inscribe themselves on maps and geopolitical discourses. They stick to some bodies more than others (Ahmed 2014). They mark what we might consider a form of "slow violence" against Indigenous peoples in the North, where residents were and are still displaced, relocated and disappear (Nixon 2013). While there is no shortage of stories about a "new North" and how climate change will transform the geophysical and geopolitical boundaries of the Arctic, we might pause and listen to others as they express their unease with past, current and possibly future borders, and the border-work that accompanies these assemblages (Stuhl 2016). The Arctic border is not and never has been simply a line on the earth, water and ice, let alone the map. As the mythical Greek river god Scamander recognised, borders like rivers have the capacity to be displaced, unsettled and disturbed.

References

Abele, F. 2016. "The North in New Times: Revising Federal Priorities". Pp. 5-11 in *North of 60: Toward a Renewed Canadian Arctic Agenda*, edited by J. Higginbotham and J. Spence. Waterloo, ON: Centre for International Governance Innovation.

Ahmed, S. 2014. *The Cultural Politics of Emotion* Edinburgh: Edinburgh University Press.

Arctic Council's Conservation of Arctic Fauna and Flora (CAFF). 2017. *Arctic Invasive Alien Species Strategy and Action Plan (2017).* https://www.caff.is/strategies-series/415-arctic-invasive-alien-species-strategy-and-action-plan.

Anker, E. 2013. "In the Shadowlands of Sovereignty: The Politics of Enclosure in Alejandro Gonzalez Inarritu's Babel." *University of Toronto Quarterly* 82(4): 950-73.

Baker, A. 2009. "The contemporary reality of Canadian imperialism: Settler colonialism and the hybrid colonial state." *The American Indian Quarterly* 33(3): 325-51.

Benton, L. 2009. *A Search for Sovereignty.* Cambridge: Cambridge University Press.

Burke, D. 2017. "Leading by example: Canada and its Arctic stewardship role." *International Journal of Public Policy* 13(1/2): 36-52.

Byers, M. *International Law and the Arctic.* Cambridge: Cambridge University Press.

Cameron, E. 2016. *Far Off Metal River: Inuit Lands, Settler Stories, and the Making of the Contemporary Arctic.* Vancouver: University of British Columbia Press.

CBC News. 2017. "Over 3000 indigenous lands added to Google Maps, Earth." June 21. https://globalnews.ca/news/3546031/over-3000-indigenous-lands-added-to-google-maps-earth/.

CBC Radio. 2017. "Inuk performance artist challenges 'Southern Canadians' on their perceptions of 'the North'." July 2. http://www.cbc.ca/radio/outintheopen/hyphen-state-1.4184855/inuk-performance-artist-challenges-southern-canadians-on-their-perceptions-of-the-north-1.4184921?cmp=rss.

"A Circumpolar Inuit Declaration on Sovereignty in the Arctic." 2009. http://www.inuitcircumpolar.com/sovereignty-in-the-arctic.html.

De Leon, J. 2015. *The Land of Open Graves.* Berkeley, CA: University of California Press.

Dodds, K. 2010. "Flag waving and finger pointing: The Law of the Sea, the Arctic and the political geographies of the outer continental shelf." *Political Geography* 29(2): 63-73.

_____. 2013. "The Ilulissat Declaration (2008): The Arctic States, "Law of the Sea," and Arctic Ocean." *SAIS Review of International Affairs* 33(2): 45-55.

Dodds, K. and Nuttall, M. 2016. *The Scramble for the Poles.* Cambridge: Polity.

"How we misunderstand the Canadian North." 2014. *Globe and Mail,* January 20. https://www.theglobeandmail.com/news/national/the-north/arctic-circle-panel-how-we-misunderstand-the-canadian-north/article16404201/?page=all

Griffiths, F. 1987. *Politics of the Northwest Passage* Kingston and Montreal: McGill-Queens University Press.

"The Ilulissat Declaration." 2008. Arctic Ocean Conference. Ilulissat, Greenland. http://www.oceanlaw.org/downloads/arctic/Ilulissat_Declaration.pdf.

Jensen, O. 2015. "Maritime Boundary Delimitation Beyond 200 Nautical Miles: The International Judiciary and the Commission on the Limits of the Continental Shelf." *Nordic Journal of International Law* 84(4): 580-604.

Johnson, C., Jones, R., Paasi, A., Amoore, L., Mountz, A., Salter, M., and Rumford,

C. 2011. "Interventions on rethinking "the border" in border studies." *Political Geography* 30(2): 61–9.

Jones R., and Johnson, C. 2016. "Border militarization and the re-articulation of sovereignty." *Transactions of the Institute of British Geographers* 41(2): 187-200.

Lackenbauer, W. and Farish, M. 2007. "The Cold War on Canadian soil: Militarizing a northern environment." *Environmental History* 12(4): 920-50.

Lajeunesse, A. 2016. *Lock, Stock and Icebergs: A History of Canadian Arctic Maritime Sovereignty.* Vancouver: UBC Press.

McGhee, R. 2008. *The Last Imaginary Place: A Human History of the Arctic.* Chicago: University of Chicago Press.

Milloy, S. 1999. *A National Crime: The Canadian Government and the Residential School System.* Winnipeg: University of Manitoba Press.

Neyers, P. 2012. "Moving borders: the politics of dirt." *Radical Philosophy* 174. https://www.radicalphilosophy.com/commentary/moving-borders

Nicol, H. 2010. "Reframing sovereignty: Indigenous peoples and Arctic States." *Political Geography* 29(2): 78-80.

Nicol, H. 2015. *The Fence and the Bridge: Geopolitics and Identity along the Canada-US Border.* Waterloo, ON: Wilfrid Laurier Press.

Nixon, R. 2013. *Slow Violence and the Environmentalism of the Poor.* Cambridge, MA: Harvard University Press.

Panquin, J. and James, P. 2014. *Game Changer: The Impact of 9/11 on North American Security.* Vancouver: University of British Columbia Press.

Phaneuf, R. 1979. "Indian reserve boundaries and rights: enforcement of the St. Lawrence River." *Canadian Water Resources Journal* 4(3): 30-4.

Porter, J. 1965. *The Vertical Mosaic: An Analysis of Social Class and Power in Canada.* Toronto: University of Toronto Press.

Powell, R. 2010. "Lines of possession? The anxious constitution of a polar geopolitics." *Political Geography* 29(2): 74-7.

Rothwell, D. and Stephens, T. 2016. *The International Law of the Sea.* Oxford: Hart.

Steinberg, P., Tasch, J., and Gerhardt, H. 2015. *Contesting the Arctic: Politics and Imaginaries in the Circumpolar North.* London: I B Tauris.

Steinberg, P. and Peters, K. 2015. "Wet Ontologies, Fluid Spaces: Giving Depth to Volume through Oceanic Thinking." *Environment and Planning D: Society and Space* 33(2): 247-64.

Steinberg, P. and Kristoffersen, B. 2017. "The ice edge is lost … nature moved it": mapping ice as state practice in the Canadian and Norwegian North" *Transactions of the Institute of British Geographers* 42(4): 625-41.

Stuhl, A. 2016. *Unfreezing the Arctic: Science, Colonialism and the Transformation of Inuit Lands.* Chicago: University of Chicago Press.

Thobani, S. 2007. *Exalted Subjects: Studies in the Making of Race and Nation in Canada.* Toronto: University of Toronto Press.

Truth and Reconciliation Commission of Canada. 2015. *Honouring the Truth, Reconciling for the Future: Final Report of the Truth and Reconciliation Commission of Canada.* http://www.trc.ca/websites/trcinstitution/index.php?p=890.

UNCLOS. 1982. The United Nations Law of the Sea Convention. http://www.un-.org/depts/los/convention_agreements/texts/unclos/unclos_e.pdf

Wilson Center. 2014. "I didn't know that! Arctic borders are still not settled." https://www.wilsoncenter.org/publication/arctic-borders-still-arent-settled.

CHAPTER FIVE

Securitization along Canada's Southern Border

Emily Gilbert

Hardening the Canada-US Border

One of President Donald Trump's key campaign promises was to build a wall at the Mexico-US border,[1] fanning fears of terrorism and job theft. Whether a wall will be constructed is still in question. Congress has not yet allocated the required funds, estimated at more than $21 billion.[2] Nor has Mexico agreed to pay for construction, despite Trump's promise during the election that he would compel them to do so. However, even if the wall is never built, increased securitization and even militarization of the US-Mexico border has taken place over the last two decades and is ongoing. Under the direction of successive governments since the attacks against the United States on 11 September 2001, new forms of surveillance and patrolling have been implemented, from the use of Predator drones repurposed from their use in Afghanistan to the increased deployment of the National Guard (Jones and Johnson 2016).

For now, the same kind of pressure has not been directed at the Canada-US border. Trump has stated that a wall along the US northern border is not necessary. Yet the idea of a border fence has been floated by some. During the US presidential campaign, Republican candidate Scott Walker called the building of a northern wall a "legitimate" issue. While the proposal was widely criticized on social media, and Walker ended his campaign soon thereafter, some polls suggest that more than 40 percent of Americans would support building a wall along the northern border (CBC News 2015). The Department of Homeland Security has also repeatedly stated that while there are multiple threats at the US-Mexico border, the Canada-US border poses more of a security threat because of its rela-

---

1. Already, about one-third of the 3,058 km border with Mexico is fenced with single, double and triple fence; Trump's proposal is to secure the remaining 2,006 km.
2. US dollars throughout.

tive openness (Department of Homeland Security 2015). Although a physical barrier has not been built nor is anticipated, securitization has increased at the Canada-US border, much of it rationalized as a counter-terrorism effort, especially through more intensive forms of surveillance (Gilbert 2012). The number of border agents has gone up. More surveillance cameras have been installed. Drones now patrol the border airspace. Indeed, Peter Andreas (2005) suggests that heightened security since 9/11 has resulted in a "Mexicanization" of the Canada-US border.

As I will illustrate, the effect of increased surveillance has been dramatic, both for those attempting to cross the border and for the communities situated in the border's shadow. Significantly, however, the securitization of the border is also taking place through changes to immigration and refugee legislation. For example, the Safe Third Country Agreement (STCA), which came into effect in 2004, limits the movement of asylum seekers across the Canada-US border. In the wake of the election of President Trump, the STCA has received significant attention as vulnerable populations are looking to leave the United States in the face of the government's overt racism and xenophobia. Many have made their way to Canada in the hope of claiming asylum. However, under the terms of the STCA such asylum seekers cannot present themselves at official ports of entry, and have thus been compelled to find irregular ways to cross the border. As I will discuss below, the result is that these border-crossers are rendered even more vulnerable.

I also examine other ways that Canada and the US are collaborating on border security so as to pull border functions away from the border. These initiatives have been designed to take pressure off the border while not removing it as a final line of defense, thus helping to smooth movement of the $2 billion in goods and services that cross the border daily. Canada's economy is especially dependent on this trade, which is why Canada has eagerly proposed and embraced initiatives that ensure more efficient border functions. I focus on two such initiatives: the expansion of customs pre-clearance programs, and new forms of cross-border law enforcement. Each of these initiatives is reworking ideas of territorial jurisdiction and national sovereignty, with significant implications for authority and accountability.

In short, the hardening of the Canada-US border through increased security and surveillance is taking place alongside deepening cooperation and collaboration. Borders are not simply about keeping people out, although that is certainly one way that they are used. Rather, borders are used to control circulation of people and things, to moderate who and what is allowed through, and under what terms (Pallister-Wilkins 2016). Moreover, legal and jurisdictional changes are being introduced so that "the border itself has become a moving barrier, a legal construct that is not tightly fixed to territorial benchmarks" (Shachar 2009: 811). I address these complexities at the Canada-US border in what follows. By way of conclusion I ask whether the new intensity of securitization is necessary.

Border Security, Border Surveillance

Borders are being fortified and militarized around the world (Jones and Johnson 2016). Border fences or walls have been built between South Africa and Zimbabwe; Saudi Arabia and Yemen; India and Pakistan, Bangladesh, Burma and Kashmir; Turkmenistan and Uzbekistan; Botswana and Zimbabwe; Thailand and Malaysia; Egypt and Gaza; Israel and the West Bank and Gaza; Iran and Pakistan; Brunei and Limbang District; and China and North Korea (Brown 2010). Border controls were reintroduced temporarily in some parts of the Schengen Area[3]—including Austria, Belgium, Denmark, France, Germany, Norway and Sweden—to stop or control the entry of refugees. Some European countries, including Croatia, Hungary, Serbia, Slovenia, and the Spanish enclaves of Melilla and Ceuta in Morocco, have also hardened their external borders by erecting fences. In many cases this construction is not just about building walls: "Deployment of new unmanned aerial systems (UAVs, or drones), sophisticated surveillance systems, high-tech sensors, along with military hardware, including attack helicopters and armoured vehicles, represents an even more widespread trend" (Jones and Johnson 2016: 187).

Ironically for an era that has been proclaimed an age of globalization, there are more walls and fences in the world today than there were during the Cold War (Jones and Johnson 2016: 187; Vallet and David, 2012). As the world has become more interconnected through trade, transportation and communication, more attempts have been made to limit the movement of people. The rationale is often one of security, although who is being secured, and from what, varies from undesirables to weapons, drugs, insects, and pathogens (Brown 2010: 20). Those who are most at risk are bearing the brunt of these changes, for as more people seek to cross borders to save their lives, more obstacles are put in their way.

3. The Schengen Agreement of 1985 led to the removal of border controls among signatory nations; as of 2017, 26 European countries were members of the Schengen Area.

Securitization is also on the increase at the Canada-US border. Since the terrorist attacks of 9/11, the two countries have worked together, mostly bilaterally but sometimes also with Mexico, to make the border less permeable.[4] This effort has included a range of measures. The number of US border agents has jumped more than sixfold from 340 in 2001 to about 2,200 in 2016. In 2009, Canada made the decision to arm its border agents. New technologies have been implemented, from full body x-ray scanners at international airports to radio frequency identification and radiation-detection technologies at select land borders. Sixteen surveillance towers have been erected in the Detroit and Buffalo areas to monitor the regions' border waterways. The United States has located five air and marine bases near the northern border to undertake surveillance, including by unmanned Predator drones, repurposed from their incursions in the Middle East. Canada has announced a new Border Integrity Technology Enhancement Project, which is now being implemented along a 700 km route from Oakville, Ontario, to the Quebec-Maine border. Anticipated to be completed in 2018, this $92 million surveillance web will consist of Royal Canadian Mounted Police (RCMP) video cameras, radar, ground sensors, thermal radiation detectors, and other surveillance technologies. The plan is for the system to be interoperable with the United States in due course.

The impact of securitization is experienced viscerally by those living in adjacent communities, such as Derby Line, Vermont, and Stanstead, Quebec. Before 9/11 it was possible to cross the border simply by crossing the street—perhaps to borrow a lawnmower or a cup of sugar—without needing to report to customs. Not now. Access is blocked by gates that create barriers between neighbours and prevent cross-border vehicular and pedestrian traffic. Surveillance cameras have proliferated, as have border agents.

To show that border agents mean business, Roland "Buzzy" Roy, an American pharmacist, was arrested in 2010 and levied a $500 fine when he crossed into Canada to buy a pizza without reporting to

4. Notably, border security since 9/11 has largely been dealt with bilaterally, rather than within the NAFTA framework. There was a move towards trilateralism with the Security and Prosperity Partnership negotiated in March 2005, which included Mexico. The agreement contained many of the same features of the Canada-US Smart Border Accord (and a similar agreement that the US had signed with Mexico in 2002). However, the trilateral agreement was short-lived; its market-based thrust towards harmonization, with no political infrastructure, democratic accountability, or public consultation or participation, was strongly opposed (Gilbert, 2007). Since then, there has been a return to bilateral approaches, as the US has signed separate border agreements with both Canada and Mexico.

customs (Yahm 2016). Despite a public campaign to support Buzzy, the charges held.

Border agents are now stationed outside the Haskell Free Library and Opera House. The building straddles the border. Completed in 1904, it was built in recognition of the friendship between the two communities. The stage is in Canada, the seats in the US; the library entrance is in the US, the books in Canada. It is still possible to navigate the building freely, and while one can enter the library on the US side without passing through US customs, the border guards are there to ensure that visitors return the way they arrived. The level of scrutiny, and efforts to thwart cross-border interactions, have dramatically reshaped the communities.

Another community heavily impacted by securitization is the Mohawk Nation at Akwesasne. The area has been called a jurisdictional nightmare because the community is bisected by the international border, with each side having its own governance structure: the Mohawk Council of Akwesasne on the Canadian side, and the St. Regis Mohawk tribe on the United States side (Mohawk Council of Akwesasne 2014). The community is also divided by three subnational authorities: the provinces of Ontario and Quebec in Canada, and the state of New York in the United States. It is additionally complicated by the fact that it straddles the St. Lawrence River. The international border has been a bane to the community since it was first imposed, without concern for the ways that it ruptured kin and governance structures. The added security since 9/11 has further strained the community. Tensions came to a head in 2009 when the Canadian Border Services Agency (CBSA) announced that it was going to arm its border agents. The CBSA post was located in the middle of the Akwesasne community, on Cornwall Island, near shops, schools and daycare centres. Many in the community were worried about the increased possibility of gun violence. On 31 May 2009, the area around the CBSA port of entry building was occupied and the bridge to the Island was barricaded to prevent through traffic. That night, the CBSA abandoned its post, and for six weeks the Canadian border crossing was closed.

The CBSA eventually relocated their operations off the island, in the town of Cornwall, outside of Akwesasne territory. The move was meant to be temporary but nine years later the border station remains in Cornwall. While the relocation removed border agents from Mohawk lands, it has also created a number of problems. People travelling from the United States to Canada are no longer able to stop and shop but must travel directly through the community to report to the customs office in the city of Cornwall. Since much of the traffic is heading to other places, it does not return to the centre of the community after customs clearance. As a result, shops and restaurants have closed. The new regime has also created difficulties for daily life in the community. For example, to get from the popular lacrosse field in Ontario to the band council office in St. Regis, Quebec, one must traverse the international boundary twice. Residents are required to check in with border authorities each time they cross the line, driving to the City of Cornwall to report, before they can drive back into the community. The duty to report is burdensome but failing to report is a criminal offence.

The stakes became clear when two Akwesasne women, both living on the Mohawk reserve in the United States, challenged the need to check in at the Cornwall border post and were charged for failing to report. In August 2011, Alicia Shenandoah dropped off her 6-year old daughter and cousin for a lacrosse match. In January 2013, Elaine Thompson dropped off her daughter and husband in Canada before reporting to CBSA. Although the women reported as required, criminal charges were laid for "aiding and abetting a person to enter Canada without appearing for examination by a border officer" because they did not go directly to the customs office. The Ontario judge who presided over the cases ruled that the inconvenience presented by the duty to report posed was minimal and was needed for national security. The charges against the women held but they received conditional discharges for six months, the minimum penalty allowed.

This ruling exemplifies the burden of the border that is borne by borderland communities. While occurring in the midst of increased securitization, these examples remind us that the violence of the border, which separates kin and impedes the exercise of sovereign autonomy, is the result of a long legacy of colonialism and state building (Walia 2013). Donald Grinde (2002: 178) asserts that, for the Iroquois, "the border serves foremost as a symbol of their oppression by colonizing national governments that have sought to destroy and/or to ignore their existence. The border for the Iroquois people is an 'unnatural notion' and will continue to be a point of protest and contention as long as it hinders the free passage of the Iroquois through their traditional homeland." These tensions are poised to increase. The recently announced RCMP Border Integrity Technology Enhancement Project will be implemented on Mohawk land. Yet consultation with Indigenous communities has not taken place, and the project is thus seen as a threat to the community's sovereignty and human rights (Mohawk Council of Akwesasne 2014).

Securitization by Other Means: The Safe Third Country Agreement

Since the election of Trump, the bilateral Safe Third Country Agreement (STCA) has regularly been in the news. The STCA was first announced in the Smart Border Accord signed between Canada and the United States just months after the terrorist attacks of 9/11 and came into effect in 2004.[5] Under its provisions, asylum seekers arriving by land must make a claim in the first "safe" country of arrival. This means that an asylum seeker cannot arrive in the United States and then make her way to Canada to seek refugee status. The claim must be made in the United States. The policy applies only at the land border at official ports of entry, with a few exceptions (for example, unaccompanied minors and those with relatives already across the border).

The STCA is effectively a mechanism for Canada to harden its refugee policies and bring them more in line with the US. Since the vast majority of asylum seekers arrive in the US first, making their way over land from Mexico or other parts of Latin America, the STCA disproportionately applies to arrivals in Canada. Effectively, the agreement is designed to prevent asylum seekers from making a claim in the US, and if refused, from trying again in Canada, which has tended to approve more refugee claims than the US does (Macklin 2005). Indeed, after its implementation, the number of refugee claimants at Canadian land borders dropped dramatically. For these reasons, Efrat Arbel argues that the STCA undermines the "very foundations" of Canada's refugee system in that it imposes limitations that are not sanctioned by the United Nations as to who is able to claim asylum (Arbel 2013: 86). It is in keeping with a widespread trend towards the securitization of migration, underway since at least the 1990s but heightened since 9/11, whereby non-nationals, especially racialized populations, are viewed as threats to national security and livelihoods (Pratt 2005).

Attempts to declare the STCA illegal and unconstitutional were launched soon after its implementation. It was argued that the STCA functioned as a kind of interdiction, rendering it impossible to make claims, or what Jennifer Hyndman and Alison Mountz have called "neo-refoulement." Refoulement is the practice whereby asylum seekers are returned to "transit countries or regions of origin before they reach the sovereign territory in which they could make a claim"

5. Discussions about implementing a safe third country agreement had begun in the 1990s, but the political willpower to move ahead did not exist at that time.

(Hyndman and Mountz 2008: 250). The practice contravenes the UN Refugee Convention. The Federal Court agreed with this assessment when it ruled on the case in 2007, also arguing that the United States could not be considered a safe country given that it was falling short on its provisions for refugees (Arbel 2013: 79). For example, women facing domestic violence and those who are LGBTQ have faced particular impediments in their asylum claims in the United States (Macklin 2005). The Federal Court even found the STCA to contravene sections 7 and 15 of the Canadian Charter of Rights and Freedoms regarding life, liberty, and security of the person, and on equality before and under the law (Arbel 2013: 66). However, this finding was overturned by the Federal Court of Appeal, which reinstated the STCA.

In July 2017, another legal challenge was lodged against the STCA by the Canadian Council for Refugees, the Canadian Council of Churches, and Amnesty International. The litigants claim that, under Trump, the United States cannot be considered a safe country because of ongoing verbal attacks on immigrants, Latinos, Muslims, and so on, which the President has backed up by proposals for a wall at the Mexican border, deportation raids, and executive order prohibitions against migrants from some Muslim-majority countries. Indeed, in 2017, about 15,000 asylum seekers crossed into Canada from the US irregularly, sometimes in dangerous circumstances, unable to enter at an official port-of-entry because of the STCA. For example, Seidu Mohammed (age 24) and Razak Iyal (age 35), both originally from Ghana, crossed into Manitoba through farmers' fields to make refugee claims. Both claims were eventually approved, but both men lost most of their fingers to frostbite, incurred when they became lost for several hours. It is not only winter weather that threatens; in June 2017, 57-year-old Mavis Otuteye, also from Ghana, was found dead near the Emerson, Manitoba crossing—tragically, she would have been eligible to enter at an official port of entry since she had immediate family already living in Canada.

Despite these horrific events, Prime Minister Trudeau has shown no inclination to rescind the STCA, even though his government has sought to project a pro-refugee stance. Canada revelled in the international attention it received when the Liberal Party welcomed 47,000 Syrian refugees in 2016–17, far exceeding the 1,200 who had been welcomed by the previous government (Gilbert 2016). While the government's commitment to Syrians waned in 2017, Trudeau has continued to insist that Canada is open to refugees. This stance was typified in the widely circulated tweet he posted after Trump announced an executive order to limit migrants from seven Muslim-majority countries and put a four-month hold on refugee claims: "To those fleeing persecution, terror & war, Canadians will welcome you, regardless of your faith. Diversity is our strength. #WelcomeTo-Canada."

The welcome is limited and politically expedient. The STCA fits Canada's immigration policies, which tend to emphasize managed migration, as in the case of the Syrian refugees, who had to pass through health and security screenings and assessments for their potential social integration before being accepted. Retaining the STCA also maintains good relations with the United States on border security, especially at a time fraught with renegotiations over the North American Free Trade Agreement (NAFTA). Trudeau's refusal to reconsider the STCA is a reminder that refugee and immigration policy is not only about making sovereign decisions about who can cross one's borders, but also about geopolitical jockeying (Mountz forthcoming). To this end, the two countries have reached a slew of other agreements on sharing information about immigrants and travellers, including the Entry/Exit initiative and the introduction of comparable reporting requirements on non-visa border crossers (the Electronic System for Travel Authorization in the United States and the Electronic Travel Authorization in Canada).

Paradoxically, the security principle at the heart of the STCA makes asylum seekers at the land border more insecure, precisely at a moment when their numbers are on the rise. In the second half of 2017, the number of border crossers from Haiti jumped as Trump announced that by July 2019 he would rescind Temporary Protective Status (TPS) for the 58,000 Haitians living and working in the United States, thus threatening their deportation. He did so despite the unsafe conditions that persist in Haiti due to the devastating 2010 earthquake, subsequent hurricanes, and the outbreak of cholera. Even before the TPS announcement, up to 200 Haitians were making their way to Canada daily, although the Trudeau government had terminated its own temporary protections in 2016 and resumed deportations. Montreal's Olympic stadium was opened as a temporary shelter, and refugee tents were set up by the Canadian Armed Forces near the Lacolle border crossing in Quebec. Winterized trailers replaced military tents in preparation for winter and the potential of another surge in asylum seekers as Trump threatened to rescind TPS for other groups, including Nicaraguans, Hondurans, and the nearly 200,000 El Salvadorans who have been in the United States since 2001 and who have about 190,000 US-born children.

Protective status has also expired on Guinea, Liberia, and Sierra Leone. If Trump ends the Deferred Action for Childhood Arrivals (DACA) program, another 800,000 people who were brought to the United States by their parents before their sixteenth birthday will also face the threat of deportation. Many of them might consider seeking asylum in Canada.

While the media have often characterized Canada's response to irregular asylum seekers as benign and benevolent, with images of RCMP officers helping them across snowy culverts, the government has undertaken concerted efforts to stifle this movement. Immigration Minister Ahmed Hussen, himself a former refugee from Somalia, as well as Spanish-speaking and Creole-speaking federal ministers, have travelled to California, Florida, Minnesota, New York, and Texas to dissuade Haitians from travelling to Canada. Most Haitians have entered Quebec, which already has a large Haitian population, and the province sent its Haitian-born MLA, Emmanuel Dubourg, to the United States to dissuade asylum seekers. The federal government launched a digital campaign to reach TPS-affected communities and caution them against travelling to Canada. For his part, Trudeau has insisted that Canada is a country of laws, that due process must be followed, and that asylum seekers gain no advantage by entering the country irregularly (Lampert 2016). Such statements echo a similar government crackdown against Haitian migrants in the mid-1970s, when the government insisted on its right to determine who enters the country in terms of the "integrity of its laws and the interests of its population" (Mills 2013: 431).

While the government refers to legality and due process, it is important to note that under the terms of the UN Refugee Convention, to which Canada is a signatory, refugee status cannot be determined by how one travels, nor is it illegal to make an irregular crossing. Indeed, it is recognized that in many cases this is the only option available to an asylum seeker. Thus, the STCA contravenes the spirit of asylum and makes refugees more vulnerable by exposing them to increased risk. However, the agreement is politically expedient for Canada insofar as it expresses Canada's commitment to a hard line on asylum seekers and brings the country's immigration and refugee policies more in line with those of the United States, thereby reinforcing the notion that issues of mobility are primarily ones of security. The problematic aspects of this cooperation are especially apparent when we examine the new kinds of cross-border law enforcement that are in place between the two countries.

Beyond the Border

Within months of the 9/11 terrorist attacks, Canada and the United States had signed a sweeping new border agreement. The Canada-US Smart Border Accord was negotiated "to develop a zone of confidence against terrorist activity" by creating a border that would allow the free flow of "legitimate" trade and people but make the border more impermeable to threats (Gilbert 2005). Doing so would require deeper collaboration between the two countries on issues such as cargo screening, investment in infrastructure, and the harmonization of immigration and refugee policy, all of which would involve more intensive and extensive forms of information sharing. The objective of these measures was to bolster security while also facilitating the extensive cross-border trade that is important to both economies, but upon which Canada in particular relies. The "Beyond the Border" agreement, announced in February 2011 by Prime Minister Stephen Harper and President Barack Obama, continued in this vein and encouraged even more cooperation and collaboration. For Harper, the Beyond the Border agreement was the "most significant step forward in Canada-US co-operation since the North American Free Trade Agreement" (Payton 2015).

The United States Department of Homeland Security website declares: "*Beyond the Border* articulates a shared approach to security in which both countries work together to address threats within, at, and away from our borders, while expediting lawful trade and travel" (Department of Homeland Security 2011). Such deterritorialization, reterritorialization, and extra-territorialization of borders has become commonplace, and while it was underway before 9/11, the heightened security context has been used to intensify these processes.

Much of the focus has been on what is taking place in Europe and Australia. The countries of the European Union's Schengen Area have not only externalized their border controls but have seen them relocate to countries in their periphery (Vaughan-Williams, 2015; Zaotti 2016). Examples include Italy's detention centre on the Mediterranean island of Lampedusa (Andrijasevec 2010) and the EU's offshoring and outsourcing of border controls to Libya and other parts of North Africa and the Sahel (Bialasiewicz 2012; Andersson 2014; Casas-Cortes et al. 2016). In Australia, much attention has been directed to the Pacific Solution, which has excised some islands territorially so no refugee claims can be made from them, while also offshoring detention centres to neighbouring countries (Perera 2007; Mountz 2012). In many of these cases, the complicated jurisdiction of the sea is used to legalize interception of migrants and their subsequent detention and processing offshore (Mountz and Hiemstra 2012).

As the voluminous literature shows, borders are being stretched. But like an elastic band, they are also snapping back into place (Gilbert, 2018). Said differently, border controls are being extended while the border itself becomes more hardened to the mobility of people. At the same time, cross-border agents carry with them the laws of their home countries, pulling their jurisdiction beyond its traditional territorial borders and troubling notions of national sovereignty. We can see this with the move to increased customs preclearance as set out in the Beyond the Border agreement. Canada has had customs preclearance at Toronto's Pearson airport since the 1950s, an arrangement that was formalized in the 1970s and renegotiated in the 1990s. Currently, the program is in place at eight of Canada's international airports. The principle is that travellers to the United States clear US customs in Canada before boarding their flight. As passengers do not have to go through customs upon arrival in the United States, it expedites travel: a boon when one has a connecting flight. The system also allows travellers to catch flights to domestic terminals in the United States that lack customs facilities. The added advantage from the point of view of the United States is that suspect travellers can be prevented from boarding a flight, so they never set foot on US soil, where they would be able to make an asylum claim or have access to more rights and due process. Thus, for the United States, preclearance provides an added layer of security, while for travellers preclearance is largely a question of efficiency and convenience.

Under the Beyond the Border agreement, customs preclearance will be expanded to three other Canadian international airports and to some bus terminals, train stations, and ports that provide direct routes to the United States. (There are also provisions in the agreement for Canadian customs preclearance to be set up in the United States, but no proposals along these lines have been announced.) Both Canada and the US have passed legislation to govern how preclearance is operationalized. Under the terms of Canada's *Bill C-23: An Act respecting the preclearance of persons and goods in Canada and the United States*, agents at the United States border will have greatly expanded rights. For one, they will be armed—something that was not permitted under previous preclearance directives. This is particularly concerning given that the new sites where preclearance will take place—bus and train stations, and some ferry ports—

are central transportation hubs where local passengers, workers, and transient populations assemble and are on the move. It means that foreign agents will be carrying weapons in some of the most highly populated and dynamic urban spaces in the country.

Bill C-23 also permits US border agents to detain travellers indefinitely as long as their detention is not deemed "unreasonable." Whereas one used to be able to withdraw from customs procedures without penalty, now the decision not to travel can be treated as suspect. It can be grounds for detention—until the suspicion is cleared—and denial of future entry to the United States. Agents of the US Customs and Border Patrol will also be allowed to conduct strip searches when a Canadian official is unavailable or chooses not to participate for whatever reason. Finally, according to the new legislation, the language around the use of force has changed. Whereas previously border agents were "authorized" to use "as much force as is necessary," they are now "justified" in doing so. As these examples make clear, the rights of border enforcement have been much expanded under this legislation.

In contrast, the rights of travellers have diminished. While an amendment to Bill C-23 now permits "administrative remedy" for travellers who are mistreated, the decisions of the US Customs and Border Patrol cannot be appealed. Furthermore, under legislation passed in the US (*Bill HR4657: Promoting Travel, Commerce and National Security Act of 2016*), border agents operating in Canada can only be held accountable for federal offenses in the United States. They have immunity from civil proceedings in Canada.

Taken together, the terms of Bill C-23 and Bill HR4657 limit the accountability of US border agents on Canadian soil and travellers' right to appeal. This arrangement contradicts Trudeau's assertion that expanded preclearance in Canada brings more protections for Canadians because the Canadian Charter, Bill of Rights, and Human Rights Act apply (Curry 2017). As the legislation insists, US laws, some of which may contravene Canadian standards, will be applied. Effectively, the US will be able to impose executive orders banning immigrants from Muslim-majority countries, although this kind of discriminatory legislation could well be determined to be anti-constitutional. Furthermore, more intrusive border searches— the "extreme vetting" that Trump has promised, including cell phone and laptop searches without warrant—would also be permitted by US border agents for whom the Fourth Amendment protections against warrantless searches are suspended. While the CBSA has also been authorized to undertake warrantless searches, in practice there must be grounds for them to do so, in line with Supreme Court rulings that cell phone searches are "extremely intrusive" (Therrien 2017). However, this level of accountability does not apply to the US agents, something which is especially worrying as the number of searches of electronic devices, and the capture of information on them, have skyrocketed since Trump's election.

Under the Beyond the Border agreement, extra-juridical powers are also being enacted through cross-border law enforcement. Even before 9/11 cross-border cooperation in law enforcement was growing. With the Smart Border Accord of 2001, Integrated Border Enforcement Teams (IBETs) were created. They draw together Canadian and US border enforcement agencies—the RCMP, CBSA, US Coast Guard, US Customs and Border Protection, and US Joint Task Force North—to facilitate cross-border information sharing. They operate in areas between official ports of entry.

While the IBETs stay within their own national jurisdiction, this is not the case with a new program first piloted in 2005. Colloquially called Shiprider, the agreement allows for joint vessel patrols in shared and undisputed Canada-US waterways, whether internal bodies of water or at sea (Gilbert 2013). Shiprider boats carry members of the US Coast Guard and the Canadian RCMP. As the vessel crosses the border, a "home" officer takes charge. Thus, Shiprider, as described on the RCMP website, "removes the international maritime boundary as a barrier to law enforcement by enabling seamless continuity of enforcement and security operations across the border, facilitating cross-border surveillance and interdiction, and serving as both a force multiplier and, potentially, as a model for other US/Canadian cross-border (integrated) enforcement and security initiatives" (Shiprider 2016). Limited consultation has taken place with Indigenous peoples concerning Shiprider. For this reason, the Mohawk Nation Council of Chiefs has criticized the program, which operates on the St. Lawrence River that runs through the Akwesasne reserve (Anon 2011; Pratt 2016).

To meet its obligations to cross-border law enforcement under the Beyond the Border agreement, Canada passed the *Integrated Cross-Border Maritime Law Enforcement Operations Act*, which assigns designated Shiprider personnel who cross over into Canada the powers equivalent to an RCMP officer.[6] Effectively, US agents are bestowed the right to bear arms and powers of arrest. Furthermore, the RCMP designation not only pertains to the marine operation

6. Canadian officers operating in the US are covered by the pre-existing US code Title 19.

itself but to any activity arising from it, such as subsequent court appearances. It applies equally to any backup support and could thus be extended to those providing air surveillance. All designated officers are provided with training in the laws and procedures of both countries, although the eight days that are allocated for this purpose might be deemed insufficient (Bolster, 2015).

With respect to Shiprider, the laws of the host country apply with respect to the arrest, so the situation is somewhat different from the pre-clearance scenario outline earlier. But there are parallels in the ways that US agents operating in Canada carry US legislation with them. US agents operating in Canada are not subject to the same regulations as their equivalent Canadian officers. For example, if an investigation regarding an operation were required, and if something were to go wrong, US agents would not be compelled to cooperate—as would an RCMP officer—although they would be "encouraged" to do so. The US Coast Guard or other enforcement officers involved would be held to US standards, which do not have the same oversight or disclosure laws (Harris 2013).

The complexity of maritime operations and jurisdictions has facilitated the implementation of Shiprider. Attempts to expand Shiprider into a corresponding land arrangement under the Beyond the Border agreement have been thwarted. The proposed NxtGen initiative would operate between official ports of entry and would thus expand the IBETs already in place. However, the jurisdictional problems on land are much harder to address than those on the water, where questions of sovereignty are characteristically murkier (Mountz and Hiemstra 2012). Canadian government memos released under a Freedom of Information Act request have made it clear that a sticking point was the US insistence that its cross-border agents be armed, a demand with which Canada refused to comply (CBC, 2013). However, now that provisions along these lines have been made possible through the expanded preclearance program, precedent might have been created for a land-based NxtGen to go ahead.

Is Securitization Necessary?

It is unlikely that a wall will be built at the Canada-US border in the foreseeable future, yet there is no question that securitization is well underway through an intensification of infrastructure, personnel, and technology. Securitization is also taking place through bilateral agreements on immigration such as the Safe Third Country Agreement, which limits the capacity of refugee claimants to seek asylum at the Canada-US land border. Other innovations such as customs preclearance and cross-border law enforcement are pulling border functions away from the border and remapping questions of jurisdiction, territoriality, and sovereignty in ways that limit the rights of border crossers while expanding those of border enforcement.

Is all this border security really necessary? Are the infringements on human rights and the challenge posed to national sovereignty worth it? Finding a direct answer to these questions is difficult; Canada and the United States insist that investment in border security is necessary to prevent another attack like that of 9/11, yet the pretext of national security is used to limit access to information on the degree to which border security has been effective in these ways. Certainly, there have been a few high profile cases where terrorism plots have been unearthed. In 2013, for example, two suspects were charged with planning an attack on a Via Rail train, most likely on the route from Toronto to New York. Both men were sentenced to life imprisonment in 2015. Cooperation between security agencies on either side of the border, including border agencies, helped to prevent what might have been significant casualties. Most of the time, however, the deep collaboration and integration of cross-border security is directed towards other kinds of offences such as smuggling and human trafficking. Thus, while the rhetoric and rationale is predominantly about terrorism prevention, the actual crimes that are pursued are not. While these crimes are not victimless, it is not clear that the billions of dollars that have been spent on border security are necessary to address these crimes. Nor is it clear that resources are being optimally directed.

The small number of terrorist attacks by non-nationals in North America since 9/11 has also been used to demonstrate the efficacy of border security and of keeping threats out. Trump has fuelled fears that immigrants are responsible for terrorism with his series of executive orders to reduce or forbid immigration and refugees from several Muslim-majority nations. The first of these executive orders was titled "Protecting the Nation from Foreign Terrorist Entry into the United States." Yet focusing on foreigners is disingenuous. Not only has there been a rise in "homegrown" terrorism, which undermines the association of terrorism with non-nationals, but the largest threat of violent extremism in the United States is in fact posed by domestic far right extremist groups. A US Government Accountability Office report in April 2017 notes:

Of the 85 violent extremist incidents that resulted in death since September 11, 2001, far right wing violent extremist groups were responsible for 62 (73 percent) while radical Islamist violent extremists were responsible for 23 (27 percent) (United States Government Accountability Office 2017: 4).

No deaths were caused by far left-wing groups. These figures also suggest that the extravagant costs of border security, and the increased securitization of migration, are inappropriate responses to the threat of terrorism. Given that the evidence of success is so small, it is time to reassess the degree to which resources have been allocated to border security and how securitization is eroding human rights and perpetuating narratives that criminalize migrants and refugees. In the drive to make our borders more secure, we are creating more anxiety, more uncertainty, and more insecurity.

References

Andersson, R. 2014. "Hunter and Prey: Patrolling Clandestine Migration in the Euro-African Borderlands." *Anthropological Quarterly* 87(1): 119-150.

Andreas, P. 2005. "The Mexicanization of the US-Canada Border: Asymmetric Interdependence in a Changing Security Context." *International Journal* 60(2): 449-62.

Andrijasevic, R. 2010. "From Exception to Excess: Detention and Deportations across the Mediterranean Space." Pp. 147-65 in *The Deportation Regime: Sovereignty, Space, and the Freedom of Movement*, edited by N. de Genova and N. Peutz. Durham, NC: Duke University Press.

Anonymous. 2011. "Letter to the Editor: Mohawk Nation Opposes Shiprider program," *Indian Times*, Enniska (February) 25. http://www.indiantime.net/story/2011/03/10/letters-to-the-editor/letter-to-theeditor/9252.html.

Arbel, E. 2013. "Shifting Borders and the Boundaries of Rights: Examining the Safe Third Country Agreement between Canada and the United States." *International Journal of Refugee Law* 25(1): 65-86.

Bialasiewiscz, L. 2012. "Off-Shoring and Out-Sourcing the Borders of Europe: Libya and EU Border Work in the Mediterranean." *Geopolitics* 17: 843-66.

Bolster, K. 2016. "Elite Training in North Charleston Adds to Safety of U.S. Border" *Live 5 News: The Lowcountry's New Leader*, December 16. http://www.live5news.com/story/30769471/elite-training-in-north-charleston-adds-to-safety-of-us-border.

Brown, W. 2010. *Walled States: Waning Sovereignty*. New York: Zone Books.

Casas-Cortes, M., S. Cobarrubias, and J. Pickles. 2016. "'Good Neighbours Make Good Fences': Seahorse Operations, Border Externalization and Extra-Territoriality." *European Urban and Regional Studies* 23(3): 231-251.

CBC News. 2013. "U.S. Wants Exemption from Canadian Law for Cross-Border Officers." July 31. http://www.cbc.ca/news/politics/u-s-wants-cross-border-officers-exempt-from-canadian-law-1.1359107.

CBC News. 2015. "41% of Americans Would Support a Wall on the Canadian Border: Poll." September 24. http://www.cbc.ca/news/trending/wall-canadian-border-poll-scott-walker-1.3242383.

Curry, B. 2017. "Charter will Protect Canadians at US Border Preclearance: Trudeau." *The Globe and Mail*, February 22. https://www.theglobeandmail.com/news/politics/charter-will-protect-canadians-at-us-border-prescreening-trudeau-says/article34110849/.

Department of Homeland Security. 2011. *Beyond the Border: A Shared Vision for Perimeter Security and Economic Competitiveness*. December 5. https://www.dhs.gov/beyond-border.

Department of Homeland Security. 2015. *The State of America's Border Security*. Committee on Homeland Security and Governmental Affairs, United States Senate. November 23. https://www.hsgac.senate.gov/download/the-state-of-americas-border-security.

Gilbert, E. 2005. "The Inevitability of Integration? Neoliberal Discourse and the Proposals for a New North American Economic Space after September 11." *Annals of the Association of American Geographers* 95(1): 202-22.

Gilbert, E. 2007. "Leaky Borders and Solid Citizens: Governing Security, Prosperity and Quality of Life in a North American Partnership." *Antipode* 39(1): 77-98.

Gilbert, E. 2012. "Borders and Security in North America." Pp. 196-218 in *North America in Question: Regional Integration in an Era of Economic Turbulence*, edited by J. Ayres and L. Macdonald. Toronto: University of Toronto Press.

Gilbert, E. 2013. "Many Questions with Cross-Border Policing." *Embassy: Canada's Foreign Policy Newspaper* Wednesday April 24: 23.

Gilbert, E. 2016. "Spatializing the State in Border Studies." *Political Geography* 59: 8-10.

Gilbert, E. 2018. "Elasticity at the Canada-US Border: Jurisdiction, Rights, Accountability." *Environment and Planning C: Politics and Space.* Forthcoming.

Government of Canada. 2009. *Canada's Northern Strategy: Our North, Our Heritage, Our Future*; Ministry of Indian Affairs and Northern Development and Federal Interlocutor for Métis and Non-Status Indians; Ottawa.

Grinde, D.A. 2002. "Iroquois Border Crossings: Place, Politics and the Jay Treaty." Pp. 167-182 in *Globalization on the Line: Culture, Capital, and Citizenship at US Border*, edited by C. Sadowski-Smith. New York: Palgrave.

Harris, M. 2013. "The Royal Canadian and American Mounted Police?" *iPolitics*, July 28. https://ipolitics.ca/2013/07/28/385546/.

Hyndman, J. and A. Mountz. 2008. "Another Brick in the Wall? Neo-Refoulement and the Externalization of Asylum by Australia and Europe." *Government and Opposition* 43(2): 249-69.

Jones, R. and C. Johnson. 2016. "Border Militarization and the Rearticulation of Sovereignty." *Transactions of the Institute of British Geographers* 41(2): 187-200.

Lampert, A. 2017. "Canada's Trudeau Warns against Entering Country 'Irregularly.'" *Reuters*, August 20. https://ca.reuters.com/article/topNews/id-CAKCN1B00M9-OCATP.

Macklin, A. 2005. "Disappearing Refugees: Reflections on the Canada-US Safe Third Country Agreement." *Columbia Human Rights Law Review* 36: 365-426.

Mohawk Council of Akwesasne. 2014. "MCA Responds to RCMP Surveillance Fence Announcement." November 14. http://www.akwesasne.ca/node/460.

Mills, S. 2013. "Quebec, Haiti, and the Deportation Crisis of 1974." *Canadian Historical Review* 94(3): 405-435.

Mountz, A. 2012. "Mapping Remote Detention: Dis/location Through Isolation." Pp. 91-104 in *Beyond Walls and Cages: Prisons, Borders, and Global Crisis*, edited by J.M. Loyd, M. Michelson, and A. Burridge. Athens, GA: The University of Georgia Press.

Mountz, A. Forthcoming. *The Enforcement Archipelago: Hidden Geographies and the Death of Asylum*. Minneapolis: The University of Minnesota Press.

Mountz, A. and N. Hiemstra. 2012. "Spatial Strategies for Rebordering Human Migration at Sea." Pp. 455-72 in *A Companion to Border Studies*, edited by T.M. Wilson and H. Donnan. Hoboken, NJ: Wiley-Blackwell.

Pallister-Wilkins, P. 2016. "How Walls Do Work: Security Barriers as Devices of Interruption and Data Capture." *Security Dialogue* 47(2): 151-164.

Payton, L. 2011. "Canada-U.S. Border Deal Marks 'Significant Step'" *CBC News*, December 7. http://www.cbc.ca/news/politics/canada-u-s-border-deal-marks-significant-step-1.1079546.

Perera, S. 2007. "A Pacific Zone? (In)security, Sovereignty, and Stories of the Pacific Borderscape." Pp. 201-27 in *Borderscapes: Hidden Geographies and Politics at Territory's Edge*, edited by P.K. Rajaram and C. Grundy-Warr. Minneapolis: University of Minnesota Press.

Pratt, A. 2005. *Securing Borders: Detention and Deportation in Canada*. Vancouver: UBC Press.

Pratt, A. 2016. "The Canada-US Shiprider Programme, Jurisdiction and the Crimesecurity Nexus." Pp. 249-272 in *National Security, Surveillance and Terror: Canada and Australia in Comparative Perspective*, edited by R.K. Lippert, K. Walby,

I. Warren, and D. Palmer. Switzerland: Springer.

RCMP. 2016. *Canada-U.S. Shiprider*. Royal Canadian Mounted Police, October 27. http://www.rcmp-grc.gc.ca/ibet-eipf/shiprider-eng.htm.

Shachar, A. 2009. "The Shifting Borders of Immigration Regulation." *Michigan Journal of International Law* 30(3): 809-840.

Therrien, D. 2017. Remarks by Daniel Therrien, Privacy Commissioner of Canada, Appearance before the Senate Standing Committee on National Security and Defence (SECD) on Bill C-23, an Act to Amend the *Customs Act (Preclearance)*, December 4. https://www.priv.gc.ca/en/opc-actions-and-decisions/advice-to-parliament/2017/parl_20171204/.

United States Government Accountability Office. 2017. Countering Violent Extremism: Actions Needed to Define Strategy and Assess Progress of Federal Efforts. https://www.gao.gov/assets/690/683984.pdf.

Vallet, E. and C.P. David. 2012. "Introduction: The (Re)building of the Wall in International Relations." *Journal of Borderland Studies* 27(2): 111-119.

Vaughan-Williams, N. 2015. *Europe's Border Crisis: Biopolitical Security and Beyond*. Oxford: Oxford University Press.

Walia, H. 2013. *Undoing Border Imperialism*. Oakland, CA: AK Press.

Yahm, S. 2016. "The US-Canada Border Runs Through this Tiny Library." *Atlas Obscura*, July 7. https://www.atlasobscura.com/articles/the-us-canada-border-runs-through-this-tiny-library.

Zaiotti, R. ed. 2016. *Externalizing Migration Management: Europe, North America and the Spread of 'Remote Control' Practices*. New York: Routledge.

CRITIQUE

CHAPTER SIX

What Divides But Connects, Resists But Projects?

Heather N. Nicol

Borders must be two things at once. They must operate as a conduit for the world and as a wall to protect the territorial state. Canada's contemporary border situation is no different. Its focus is on projecting and defending sovereignty while encouraging transnational and global engagement.

Each contributor to this volume understands this paradox, and each challenges conventional notions about how Canadian border management works in the 21st century in relation to flows of people, data, information, and power. Their common message is that borders in general and the Canadian border in particular are being redefined by new relationships facilitated by new forms of technology, governance, actors, and agencies. Yet each contributor sees the Canadian border through a different lens—the theoretical approach of Hannigan; the functional analysis of network flows and their governance defined by Deibert and Pauly; the critical deconstruction of international agency presented by Dodds; and the deeply contextualized approach presented by Gilbert.

While the essays raise important points regarding the future of Canada's territorial borders and personal boundaries, four omissions are evident. The essays are silent, or nearly so, concerning the management of borders in the context of neoliberal restructuring and its consequences, the affective role of cyberspace in creating securitized spaces and discourses, the historical contextualization of bordering policies and strategies within continental structures of securitization in North America, and the relationship between borders and borderlands as sites of engagement and transformation, not just disembodied social spaces. The following discussion considers these issues.

Neoliberal Governance Technologies
In his essay, Hannigan distinguishes globalists who see borders

disappearing in the face of globalization and predict a borderless world from territorialists who emphasize the increasing number of borders, the hardening of existing borders, and the overall increase in the number of territorial states. While the distinction is valid, both schools acknowledge that there is more at stake here than globalization and the state of borders themselves (Newman 2011, Nicol and Townsend-Gault 2005; Omahe 1990, 1995). Also at stake is the future of the world order and of the nation states that comprise it. For example, the territorialists demonstrated that more national borders were being created but questioned whether that meant that globalization was failing (Blake 2005, Nicol 2005, Newman 2011). They suggested instead that the rebordering process facilitates the rise of new forms of neoliberal state structure and agency. Borders, they claimed, would neither fade away nor prevent the development of a global world; they would facilitate globalization in new ways.

Accordingly, late 19th century and early 20th century border management adopted the ideology, technology, and practice of neoliberalism—its goal, to control trade and immigration, that is, the movement of people and goods, in new ways. In doing so, it created a regime for managing mobile and immobile classes in support of the neoliberal state and its economy (Sparke 2004, 2005, 2006). Sparke (2005, 153) argued that securitization and economic facilitation at the border "concern the transformation of citizenship on a continent shaped by a notably neoliberal nexus of securitized nationalism and free market transnationalism." He thus positioned border management pre-9/11 in the context of larger structures of neoliberal agency in relation to border management in North America, and more specifically within the US-Canada relationship mediated by NAFTA (cf. Nicol 2005, 2015).

It is important to understand the context and materiality of border processes in this light, that is to say, to see the border-making process between Canada and the US as reflecting a broader state of institutional and non-institutional responses to changing world orders, political structures, and economic relationships. The insertion of a neoliberal critique into the theorization of borders during the late 20th century and early 21st century leads to a more complete analysis of the complicity between border management technologies, governance strategies, and neoliberalism, all of which developed in tandem. Changing technologies had agency in that they helped to restructure the management of mobility but the appearance of biometric border management was an outcome that facilitated but did not cause neoliberal border management. It was symptomatic of the way in which state agency and sovereignty were being reshaped by global patterns of trade and finance which, in turn, encouraged neoliberal strategies of governance. We thus need to avoid theorizing the relationship in ways that encourage what Vance (2008) has dubbed "the dichotomous perspective" and instead see contemporary borders as both walls *and* conduits (Nicol, 2015). Moreover, we need to understand the social, political, and economic frameworks within which borders exist and are transformed. Extraterritoriality and sovereignty are not just the outcome of creeping technological innovation but of profound shifts in the political, economic, and social framing of international relations.

While the globalist and territorialist debates were foundational and continued well into the 20th century (Blake 2005, Newman 2011), it was the theoretical framing of globalization through political and economic theory centred on understanding neoliberalism that built the foundations for contemporary border theory and its application to the Canada-US border. The associated restructuring of state agency it facilitated, as well as the agency of financial models of risk assessment (Vaughn-Williams 2008) coincided with growing interest in theories of governance and biopolitics. The neoliberal state and its borders emerged as the building block of the global world.

If Sparke's (2004, 2006) analysis of "chips and strips" and the biopolitical reinvention of NAFTA borders pointed to the ways in which the neoliberal state turned to new technologies that facilitated economic flows—for example, through the use of machine-readable identity cards and electronic data sets—his analysis was also concerned with the role of borders in "disciplining" North American neoliberal citizenship. However, Walters (2006) reminds us that as borders continue to be managed in deeply personal ways, through biometric data and personal histories that embody and embed borders within us, they also contribute to new forms of governance. Indeed, the importance of technologies in bordering processes is just not in the degree to which they embody or project extraterritorial borders or create hybridized and new borders but in the way they embed and facilitate larger societal relationships and modes of governance and expand the reach of authority. We have left behind systems of governance that discipline through borders as institutional spaces of enclosure and have entered a phase of bordering through control linked to communication and information technologies (Walters 2006).

Cyberspace and Securitization

Deibert and Pauly focus on the bounding effects of cyberspace within an international and national context. Their conclusion is that the effects of extraterritorial projections of power contribute to a deepening of mutual engagement that may well have counterbalancing effects on tendencies towards cyberwarfare or catastrophic cyberattacks. Territorial states rely on global networks to defend themselves and project power—making a coming cyber-Westphalia unlikely.

While Deibert and Pauly remind us that cyberspace has its limits that reflect a balance of international and domestic interests, Murikami Wood and Ball (2016) argue that cyberspace is not just a functional network of interdependent flows counterbalancing network tendencies towards Westphalianization. It is also complex and socially constructed. For example, in their analysis of "brandscapes" and surveillance, the authors note that cyberspace is an affective space, conflating social and economic space in ways that create a type of securitizing discourse: "From developments in marketing, technology, urbanism and practices of surveillance is emerging a new mode of ordering that seeks to simultaneously construct space and subjectivity." The brandscape, they argue, is an apparatus "based on neither the force of sovereign power nor the moral discipline of panopticism or the instrumental control of post-panopticism, but on affect." Moreover, "brandscapes must also be securityscapes; in order to provide material shape to dreams of safety and risk-free living, both their boundaries and their internal norms become intensely monitored and policed." In other words, cyber-surveillance has to be recognized in ways that recognize the subjective and aspirational nature of security-making itself. This includes not only geopolitical ambitions, but also the subjective meanings and materiality of citizenship, safety, and security. Accordingly, we must look more critically at the connection between border management and national security objectives.

Much as in other areas of boundary-making, Murikami Wood and Ball (2016) challenge the idea that state agency is the exclusive agency in the securitization of cyberspace and that it shapes cyberspace monolithically. There is more to understanding the creation of affective security space than firewalls, state espionage, and the projection of power by state agency. Affective securitization is also discursive and socially constructed; applying the analytical lens of brandscaping reveals how critical it is for the projection of power globally, and particularly for the Canada-US border relationship. Yet this collection is nearly silent on the issue. Its significance resides in the fact that the projection of state power relies not just on the capacity of state agencies to surveil but also on of the capacity of cyberspace to legitimize and normalize security hegemony through substantive social content. Moreover, cyberspace provides the medium for the conveyance of powerful tropes and for creating affective spaces of engagement, for universalizing US security messages and border technologies through benign social media, targeted messaging, and online cultural and entertainment content. Affective space is critical today, when the hardening of borderlines and their simultaneous territorial dispersion also requires the deployment of a compelling popular discourse concerning the idea that movement across borders is everywhere being facilitated rather than increasingly controlled.

Contextualizing Borders

Newman (2011) reminds us that, historically, border studies have been concerned with demarcation and the temporal and geographical categorization of ethnic and linguistic differences between peoples. Border studies remain concerned with "lines on the map which are then transformed into physical fences and walls on the ground" and also with "the way that the societal managers determine the nature of inclusion and exclusion" (Newman 2011, 36). Dodds' analysis of Arctic Ocean maritime boundaries, their global and local context and agency, and the complex legal and political issues at stake, reminds us that the demarcation of lines still matter, and that borders have geographical context. They remain agents of inclusion and exclusion, as well as objects for the negotiation of power relations. In this sense, borders are sticky. Yet Dodds has little to say about the historical context of stickiness in the Arctic region; and Gilbert's analysis is just as muted regarding sticky places along the southern Canada-US border.

Gilbert does contextualize her analysis of the southern border. She underscores how new policies coupled with surveillance technologies re-inscribe national borders in ways that support the projection of US state power while at the same time reifying the notion of the international boundary in ways that comply with US hegemony after 9/11. Extraterritorial border security and management practices increasingly target a broad and mobile group of citizens, making Canadians and those who wish to become Canadians more vulnerable to US political authority even within the Canadian state. Such practices are made more onerous by the increasing reach of security interventions, including extraterritorial border checks, domestic surveillance, offshore detention, and the monitoring of personal data, all facilitated by the way in which border technologies have become more pervasive, diffuse and extraterritorial.

While Gilbert's concern is with new measures, it is important to remember that the sort of agreements they reference reflect the larger syntax of the cross-border relationship. Although I do not dispute Gilbert's point about US hegemony or her concern with the ethics of its extraterritorial impact on social justice, there is a larger story here. Dodds notes that Indigenous northerners are creating institutional and discursive spaces to resist the sublimation of Arctic bordering processes to southern and global policy goals, recasting territorialization in ways that expose and resist colonization practices. The legacy of colonialism remains pronounced along the 49th parallel too (Menezes 2017). If security practices have made the border more onerous for Indigenous communities, however, this is not the sole cause of their marginalization. The difference between US and Canadian approaches to the legitimacy of the Jay Treaty, and Canada's differential recognition of "North American Indian status" (Boos 2015), has also been a significant factor. US border agents recognize Canada's Indigenous peoples as American Indians with an inherent right to transnational status. Canada does not reciprocate.

One of the tangible outcomes of current cross-border management regimes in North America is the development of a distinctive approach to the problem. Papademetriou and Collet (2011) contend that there now exist fundamental differences between EU and North American security regimes, and that the differences are evident in four areas: collecting and sharing travellers' data; using new technologies to verify individual identity; employing new technologies to monitor physical borders; and building partnerships to achieve border management goals. Moreover, a larger North American security regime includes Canada, the United States, and Mexico and it too has had an impact on Canada's southern border with the United States (Payan 2006, Konrad and Nicol 2008, Nicol 2015). Canadians have in general discouraged US decision-makers from applying the same criteria to the Canadian and Mexican borders, encouraging bilateralism rather than continental security measures. Not surprisingly, while the EU has created an overarching border agreement within a broader supranational and monetary integration project (Brexit not withstanding), North America has not. Even the Beyond the Border Agreement between Canada and the US (which replaced the failed trilateral Prosperity and Security

Partnership among Canada, the US, and Mexico) remains a limited agreement that provides departmental and agency road maps rather than common security governance.

The story of the Canada-US border relationship and the post-9/11 negotiation of borders is also a story of the way in which Canadian decision-makers, and indeed Canadians at large, have positioned and embedded themselves "in partnership" with their hegemonic southern neighbour through asymmetrical bilateral agreements, leading to specific ways of framing security arrangements. To be sure, this arrangement is sometimes a recipe for disaster. Gilbert holds that the material world of people and places has been sacrificed to larger immigration and securitization policies and points to the increasing degrees of compliance from Canada that is required by American post-9/11 security narratives. But while she notes that such policies challenge the rights of citizens and refugees alike, and should therefore be rejected by Canadians, this would be a hard sell for any policy-maker in light of the co-constituted, binational nature of such policies. Indeed, the Beyond the Border Agreement developed only after the monumental failure of the Security and Prosperity Partnership taught the Canadian government that their constituents were less interested in continental prosperity than in cutting ties with Mexican interests to facilitate a new and more self-serving bilateral border agreement with the US (Nicol 2015). The long and deep history of engagement between Canadians and Americans thus speaks to the way in which cross-border cooperation has shaped expectations of cooperation in security, trade, and governance (Konrad and Nicol 2008). Withdrawal from these structures is unlikely if not impossible.

In short, while such practices are onerous and create vulnerability, we must recognize that states cannot easily remove themselves from entangled histories. No matter how unequal, post-9/11 borders reflect the contours of an existing and ongoing binational relationship. They do not reinvent the relationship. Moreover, the Canada-US relationship has been co-constituted. Despite disagreements and differences in perspective, the current unease over the potential failure of contemporary NAFTA negotiations tells us only too well how most Canadians feel about the importance of their border relationship with their southern neighbour.

Rethinking Borderlands
The final point of silence in this collection lies in the area of the relationship between borders and borderlands. It is in these areas

that possibilities for non-conventional narratives emerge. Hannigan argues that the future may well lie in the borderlands, where the challenge is to "transform borderlands from unsettled spaces of marginality and exclusion into emergent spaces of hope. In so doing, it is imperative to conceptualize the borderland both as a site of contestation and claims-making and as a laboratory of social change."

However, by drawing our attention away from the view of borderlands as geographical spaces, Hannigan misses the opportunity to explore how borderlands have material form and are not always situated in marginal places. Whether borderlands are vulnerable or empowered rests in large measure on their geographical situation. There exists a tendency to see Canada-US borderlands as marginalized rather than highly populated regions. In fact, economies, cultures, and family connections are highly developed across the Canada-US borderline, and have been so for a long time. Evidence exists of complex cross-border regionalism all along the borderline, leading some observers to claim that connectivity across borders has been stronger than between subnational jurisdictions within each state (Boucher 2005, Brunet-Jailly 2006, Konrad and Nicol 2008).

On the other hand, border security designed to facilitate urban industrial NAFTA borders in the Canadian heartland remains deaf to the security needs of remote communities near the Canada-US border that have a relatively small volume of cross-border traffic (Nicol 2017). While Gilbert suggests that insensitivity to the needs of these borderland communities is a consequence of their social marginalization by one-size-fits-all security measures, it should be noted that insensitivity is also the outcome of market forces that work to expedite the movement of an ever larger volume of people and goods in ways that create disincentives for policy-makers to pay much attention to small, borderland communities.

Exclusive focus on borderlands as marginalized, and in terms of their potential as sites of resistance, leads one to prescribe particular actions regarding post-9/11 border practices. However, it also begs the important question of how existing cross-border structures are adapting to changes in security regimes and possibilities for transnational cooperation. Here it is worth repeating Boucher et al.'s (2016) point concerning the need for empirical analysis of specific borders and agencies. Who has clout and how can it be mustered to create regional arrangements (Brunet-Jailly 2007)? For what purposes? In the absence of securing national policies that rescind broad security measures, how can state and non-state actors marshal the agency of borderlands to resolve security vulnerabilities and the erosion of mobility?

Conclusion

Some authors in this collection are more concerned with international relations and security, others with human experience, and still others with how state agency affects the making of border policy. But in reflecting on the central question—what is the future of Canada's borders and personal boundaries?—I think there is more to be said. Current political narratives suggest that the future of Canada lies in promoting diversity, gender equality, Indigenous rights, and refuge to the marginalized, not just in this country but worldwide. Complex challenges face Canadians in achieving these goals. Recent scholarship usefully calls for empirical work to better map out the way forward. The challenge now is to test our assertions concerning the agency and effect of bordering processes so we can use national borders as avenues for greater engagement with global systems in ways that do not erode, and ideally enhance, human rights and social, political and economic justice.

References

Amoore, L. 2011. "On the Line: Writing the Geography of the Virtual Border." *Political Geography* 30: 63-4.

Balibar, Etienne 2002: *Politics and the Other Scene*, Christine Jones, James Swenson & Chris Turner, trans. London & New York: Verso.

Blake, Gerald. 2005. "Boundary permeability in perspective." Pp. 15-25 in H. Nicol and I. Townsend-Gault eds., *Holding the Line: Borders in a Global World*. Vancouver: UBC Press.

Boos, Greg, Greg McLawson and Heather Fathali. 2014. "Canadian Indians, Inuit, Métis, and Métis: An Exploration of the Unparalleled Rights Enjoyed by American Indians Born in Canada to Freely Access the United States." *Seattle Journal of Environmental Law* 4(1): 343-407.

Boucher, Christian. 2005. "Toward North American of regional cross-border communities: A look at economic integration and socio-cultural values in Canada and the United States. Policy Research Institute, Working Paper Series 002.Ottawa: Government of Canada.

Brunet-Jailly, Emmanuel. 2005 "Theorizing Borders: An Interdisciplinary Perspective." *Geopolitics* 10(4): 633-49.

Brunet-Jailly, Emmanuel 2006. "Leader survey on Canada-US cross-border regions: an analysis." Policy Research Institute, Working Paper Series 012. Ottawa: Government of Canada.

Brunet-Jailly, Emmanuel. 2007. *Borderlands—Comparing Border Security in North America and Europe*. Ottawa: University of Ottawa Press.

Côté-Boucher, Karine, Federica Infantino, and Mark B. Salter. 2014. "Border security as practice: An agenda for research." *Security Dialogue* 45(3): 195-208.

Easton, Norman Alexander. 2007. "King George Got Diarrhea: The Yukon-Alaska Boundary Survey, Bill Rupe, and the Scottie Creek Dineh." *Alaska Journal of Anthropology* 5(1): 95-118.

Konrad, Victor and Heather Nicol. 2008. *Beyond Walls: Reinventing the Canada US Border*. Farnham UK: Ashgate Press.

Lehtonen, Pinja and Pami Aalto. 2017. "Smart and secure borders through automated border control systems in the EU? The views of political stakeholders in the Member States." *Journal of European Security* 26 (2): 207-25.

Menezes, Dwayne R. 2017. "Canada, Indigenous Peoples and Northern Borders." *The Commonwealth Journal of International Affairs* 106(5): 579-81.

Mountz, A. 2011. "The Enforcement Archipelago: Detention, Haunting, and Asylum on Islands." Political Geography 30(3): 118-28.

Murakami Wood, David and Ball, Kristie. 2016. "Brandscapes of control? Surveillance, marketing and the co-construction of subjectivity and space in neo-liberal capitalism." *Marketing Theory* 13(1): 47–67.

Newman, David. 2011. "Contemporary Research Agenda in Border Studies: An Overview." Pp. 33-48, in Doris Wastl-Walter, ed. *The Ashgate Research Companion to Border Studies*. Farnham UK: Ashgate Press.

Nicol, Heather N. and P. Whitney Lackenbauer. 2017. *The Networked North: Borders and Borderlands in the Canadian Arctic Region*. Waterloo: Borders in Globalization/Centre on Foreign Policy and Federalism.

Nicol, Heather N. 2015: *The Fence and the Bridge: Geopolitics and Identity Along the Canada-US Border*. Kitchener-Waterloo: Wilfrid Laurier University Press.

Nicol, Heather N. and Ian Townsend Gault. 2005. *Holding the Line: Borders in a Global World*. Vancouver: UBC Press.

Payan, Tony 2006. *The Three US-Mexico Border Wars: Drugs, Immigration, and*

Homeland Security. Westport CT: Praeger Security International.

Rumford, C. 2011. "Seeing Like a Border." *Political Geography* 30(2): 67-9.

Ohmae, Kenechi. 1990 *The Borderless World*. New York: Harper Collins

Sparke, Matthew. 2006. "A Neoliberal Nexus: Economy, Security and the Biopolitics of Citizenship on the Border." *Political Geography* 25(2):151-80.

Sparke, Matthew. 2005. *In the Space of Theory: Postfoundational Geographies of the Nation-State*. Minneapolis: University of Minnesota Press.

Sparke, M. 2004. "Belonging in the PACE Lane: Fast Border Crossing and Citizenship in the Age of Neoliberalism." Pp. 251-83 in Joel S. Migdal, ed. *Boundaries and Belonging: States and Societies in the Struggle to Shape Identities and Local Practices*. Cambridge UK: Cambridge University Press.

Vance, Anneliese. 2008. "Strategic responses by Canadian and US exporters to increased US border security measures: A firm-level analysis." *Economic Development Quarterly* 22(3): 219-51.

Walters, W. 2006 "Border/Control." *European Journal of Social Theory* 9(2): 187-204.

Contributors

Robert Brym, FRSC, is S.D. Clark Professor in the Department of Sociology, University of Toronto. His recent research projects deal with collective and state violence in Israel and Palestine; democracy and intolerance in the Middle East and North Africa; and the social bases of 21st century social movements. His most recent book is *Sociology as a Life or Death Issue* (Nelson, 2018). He has won numerous awards for his research and teaching, most recently the *British Journal of Sociology* Prize. For his publications, visit https://utoronto. academia.edu/RobertBrym.

Ronald J. Deibert is Professor of Political Science and Director of the Citizen Lab at the Munk School of Global Affairs, University of Toronto. The Citizen Lab undertakes interdisciplinary research at the intersection of global security, ICTs, and human rights. Deibert is the author of *Black Code: Surveillance, Privacy, and the Dark Side of the Internet* (Random House 2013), as well as numerous books, chapters, articles, and reports on Internet censorship, surveillance, and cyber security. In 2013, he was appointed to the Order of Ontario and awarded the Queen Elizabeth II Diamond Jubilee Medal, for being "among the first to recognize and take measures to mitigate growing threats to communications rights, openness and security worldwide."

Klaus Dodds is Professor of Geopolitics at Royal Holloway, University of London, and a Fellow of the Royal Geographical Society. He specializes in the study of geopolitics and security, media/popular culture, and the international governance of the Antarctic and the Arctic. He is the recipient of the Philip Leverhulme Prize for his "outstanding contribution to political geography and 'critical geopolitics.'" His recent books include *Ice: The Scramble for the Poles: Contemporary Geopolitics in the Arctic and Antarctic* (Polity, 2015) and *Nature and Culture* (University of Chicago Press, 2018).

Emily Gilbert is Associate Professor at the University of Toronto. Cross-appointed in the Canadian Studies Program and the Department of Geography and Planning, her research deals with questions relating to citizenship, mobility, borders, security and militaries. She is now completing a book entitled *Beyond the Border*. For her publications, visit https://utoronto.academia.edu/EmilyGilbert/.

John Hannigan is Professor of Sociology at the University of Toronto. He specializes in cultural policy, urban political economy, and environmental sociology. His most recent books are *Disasters without Borders: The International Politics of Natural Disasters* (Polity, 2012), and *The Geopolitics of Deep Oceans* (Wiley, 2016).

Heather N. Nicol is Professor of Geography, Trent University, Peterborough, Ontario. She is a political geographer with an interest in Canada-US relations, border studies, and circumpolar regions. Her work explores crossborder relationships and the popular geopolitics and narratives that shape them. Her most recent book, *The Fence and the Bridge: Geopolitics and Identity along the Canada-US Border* (Wilfrid Laurier University Press 2015), examines the historical relationship between border security, geopolitics, US hegemony, and the Canada-US relationship.

Louis W. Pauly, FRSC, is the J. Stefan Dupré Distinguished Professor of Political Economy in the Department of Political Science and the Munk School of Global Affairs at the University of Toronto. He has published widely in the fields of international and comparative political economy, most recently on questions involving the politics of global finance and economic crisis management. For further information, see https://munkschool.utoronto.ca/pauly/.

Index

www.ingramcontent.com/pod-product-compliance
Lightning Source LLC
Chambersburg PA
CBHW050750030426
42336CB00012B/1745

* 9 7 8 1 7 7 2 4 4 1 4 2 0 *